T0358219

Cambridge Elements

Elements in Historical Theory and Practice
edited by
Daniel Woolf
Queen's University, Ontario

WRITING THE HISTORY OF GLOBAL SLAVERY

Trevor Burnard
University of Hull

CAMBRIDGE
UNIVERSITY PRESS

Shaftesbury Road, Cambridge CB2 8EA, United Kingdom

One Liberty Plaza, 20th Floor, New York, NY 10006, USA

477 Williamstown Road, Port Melbourne, VIC 3207, Australia

314–321, 3rd Floor, Plot 3, Splendor Forum, Jasola District Centre, New Delhi – 110025, India

103 Penang Road, #05–06/07, Visioncrest Commercial, Singapore 238467

Cambridge University Press is part of Cambridge University Press & Assessment, a department of the University of Cambridge.

We share the University's mission to contribute to society through the pursuit of education, learning and research at the highest international levels of excellence.

www.cambridge.org
Information on this title: www.cambridge.org/9781009467957

DOI: 10.1017/9781009406284

First published 2023

A catalogue record for this publication is available from the British Library

ISBN 978-1-009-46795-7 Hardback
ISBN 978-1-009-40627-7 Paperback
ISSN 2634-8616 (online)
ISSN 2634-8608 (print)

Cambridge University Press & Assessment has no responsibility for the persistence or accuracy of URLs for external or third-party internet websites referred to in this publication and does not guarantee that any content on such websites is, or will remain, accurate or appropriate.

Writing the History of Global Slavery

Elements in Historical Theory and Practice

DOI: 10.1017/9781009406284
First published online: October 2023

Trevor Burnard
University of Hull

Author for correspondence: Trevor Burnard, t.g.burnard@hull.ac.uk

Abstract: This Element shows that existing models of global slavery derived from sociology and modelled closely on antebellum American slavery being normative should be replaced by global slavery that is less American and more global. It argues that we can understand the global history of slavery if we connect it more closely to another important world institution – empires in ways that historicise the study of history as an institution with a history that changes over time and space. Moreover, we can learn from scholars of modern slavery and use more than we do the enormous proliferation of usable sources about the lives, experiences and thoughts of the enslaved, from ancient to modern times, to make these voices of the enslaved crucial drivers of how we conceptualise and describe the varied kinds of global slavery in world history. This title is also available as Open Access on Cambridge Core.

This Element also has a video abstract: www.cambridge.org/Burnard

Keywords: slavery, global, voices, Atlantic, historiography

ISBNs: 9781009467957 (HB), 9781009406277 (PB), 9781009406284 (OC)
ISSNs: 2634-8616 (online), 2634-8608 (print)

Contents

Introduction: What Is Slavery?

In this Element, I assess where scholarship is in regard to major themes to a crucial institution in human history, slavery, an institution at the far end of a continuum of unequal relationships in societies generally characterised by inegalitarianism and by the great majority of people, and almost all women and children, being dependent on the will of the few. Slavery has appeared in many different forms and it is not always easy to separate what slavery is from other forms of coerced labour, especially when we compare slavery over time and place. Being a slave in America, Africa, China and the Islamic world, where an incorporative form of slavery prevailed and where slavery was largely domestic, familial and based around the politics of the household, was very different from being a plantation slave in the Americas, where slavery was racially based, not designed to incorporate but exclude enslaved people into society and where the reason for enslavement was to produce desirable goods for a developing capitalist economy, which are so different as to make one wonder whether one can usefully make comparisons between slaves on a global scale.

It is just as hard to make comparisons over space. How do we compare someone enslaved in ancient Greece with the millions of people in slavery today or, more precisely, embedded in forms of coerced labour that resemble slavery? Getting consensus on what a slave is and how slavery should be defined when the study of slavery often extends beyond slavery into coerced labour and forms of dependency is close to an impossible project. One finding from this Element is thus a negative one: we do not have a broadly accepted definition of slavery. Our accepted models, drawn from sociological models and with a heavy reliance on slavery in nineteenth-century America as the norm from which all enslavement might be analysed, are no longer sufficient to study slavery in its wide global aspects. The huge expansion of studies of global slavery which have made clear how slavery and enslaved people contributed to the making of history has considerably muddied interpretative fields, making it hard to compare and contrast slavery in a global context with the degree of rigour and certainty that we would like.

But I believe that we still have ways to think of slavery as a global institution that make comparisons between kinds of slavery and types of enslaved experience possible. There are aspects of slavery which make it distinctive. The most critical of these is the ownership of one human being by another, and the ability to buy and sell the human chattel such ownership creates. A second common characteristic is the fact that generally slavery is a heritable condition passed down maternally. Such characteristics are not to be found in the more general category of coerced labour. A good definition of slavery is by Noel Lemski where he suggests that slavery is 'the enduring, violent domination of natally alienated and inherently dishonoured individuals (slaves) that are controlled by owners (masters) who are permitted in their social context to use and enjoy, sell and exchange and abuse them as property'.[1] It is property and ownership that are key here. Slavery, as David Lewis contends and as is a vital part of the important statement by the League of Nations in 1926 that slavery was 'the status or condition of a person over whom any or all of the powers attaching to the right of ownership are exercised', is dependent on the concept of ownership. If there are constraints to an owner's ability to violently dominate a slave, which is normal in many legal systems that permitted slavery, that is perfectly congruent with property law in which ownership and use under ownership is restricted.[2]

David Brion Davis summarised this point succinctly:

> The truly striking fact, given historical changes in polity, religion, technology, modes of production, family, and kinship structures and the very meaning of 'property' is the antiquity and almost universal acceptance of the *concept* of the slave as a human being who is legally owned, used, sold or otherwise disposed of as if he or she were a domestic animal.[3]

Scholars of modern slavery agree. Joel Quirk notes how slavery has been often invoked as a rhetorical device to describe numerous forms of exploitation that had some but not complete resemblance to slavery, such as 'wage slavery' and 'sex slavery'. He concludes with Kevin Bales and Jean Allain that being faithful to the 1926 League of Nations definition with ownership being central is crucial to aligning modern slavery to previous forms of historical slavery, making it distinctive and legally actionable.[4]

Nevertheless, even if there are some aspects of slavery, like ownership, which allow it to be treated as a distinct legal category, in practice it is a very varied institution. Its variety makes it imperative to treat it not as a static institution, as models drawn from sociology tend to do, but as historically contingent, constantly evolving and highly dependent on local circumstances. This Element

---

[1] Noel Lemski, 'Framing the Question: What Is a Slave Society', in Noel Lemski and Catherine M. Cameron, eds., *What Is a Slave Society? The Practice of Slavery in Global Perspective* (Cambridge: Cambridge University Press, 2018), 43.

[2] David Lewis, 'Orlando Patterson, Property and Ancient Slavery: The Definitional Problem Revisited', in John Bodel and Walter Scheidel, eds., *On Human Bondage: After Slavery and Social Death* (Oxford: Blackwell, 2017), 265–96.

[3] David Brion Davis, *Slavery and Human Progress* (New York: Oxford University Press, 1984), 13.

[4] Joel Quirk, *Unfinished Business: A Comparative Survey of Historical and Contemporary Slavery* (Paris: UNESCO, 2008), 32; Jean Allain and Kevin Bales, 'Slavery and Its Definition', in Jean Allain, ed., *The Law and Slavery: Prohibiting Human Exploitation* (Leiden: Brill, 2015), 502–12; Julia O'Connell Davidson, *Modern Slavery: The Margins of Freedom* (New York: Palgrave Macmillan, 2015).

follows the admonition of Joseph Miller that history rather than sociology is how we should treat slavery and that we should see it as a pattern of historically informed processes and practices. Miller's work is not easy to read but makes some important points that shape my understanding of how we should write about slavery in a global context. Global history is worth emphasising here, as it is a genre of history writing that has been increasingly triumphant in the twenty-first century almost to the stage where, as David Armitage provocatively decrees, 'If you are not doing an explicitly transnational, international or global project, you now have to explain *why* you are not. There is now sufficient evidence from a sufficiently wide range of historiographies that these transnational connections have been determinative, influential and shaping throughout recorded human history, for about as long as we've known about it.'[5]

Miller sees slaving as a political strategy, often used by new elites seeking to build power or who, themselves being outsiders, as in many developing states in early modern Africa, need different kinds of support to assume and maintain political power. Slavery can thus be a solution to issues of power and a revolutionary strategy to transform pre-existing institutions. Miller stresses these 'historical strategies' as being rooted in the tool of property in humans and the tool of domination in which one person can exercise theoretically unlimited power over another human. He insists that the circumstances by which these strategies occur depend on local circumstances and on change over time, meaning that the only way to study how slavery originates, develops and is structured in any place and time is through understanding the historical contexts within which such practices and processes occurred. He argues that enslaved people need to be thought of in terms of marginality, as people with less access to resources than others and he innovatively problematises the concept of what he calls 'slaving', as a historical strategy implemented by marginalised historical actors, or enslavers, to use slavery to improve their social status in relation to established hierarchies and so move from the periphery to the centre of their communities.[6]

Thus, it is only through close attention to particular historical circumstances that we can appreciate the precise nature of enslaved marginality, or what Miller calls 'isolated helplessness'.[7] Miller is especially concerned about how the tools of history might be used to analyse historically inscribed marginality: how

---

[5] Martine van Ittersum and Jaap Jacobs, 'Are We All Global Historians Now? An Interview with David Armitage', *Itinerario* 36 (2012), 16.

[6] Joseph C. Miller, 'Slaving as Historical Process: Examples from the Ancient Mediterranean and the Modern Atlantic', in Enrico Del Lago and Constantina Katsaru, eds., *Slave Systems: Ancient and Modern* (New York: Cambridge University Press, 2008), 70–102.

[7] Joseph C. Miller, *The Problem of Slavery as History: A Global Approach* (New Haven: Yale University Press, 2013), 31.

people in positions of power but insecure in those positions resorted to slavery in order to convert their own marginality into centrality. He argues that to understand slavery we should concentrate less on the paradoxical relationship between masters and the enslaved and examine the historical contexts within which slavery was shaped.[8]

It is this historically inflected approach that informs this Element. I argue that as the history of slavery has become more a part of global history, a genre of history that foregrounds connectedness, circulation and integration and is 'a form of historical analysis in which phenomena, events and processes are placed in a global context',[9] old models derived from sociology, in which one historical period – the nineteenth-century American South – served as a model of the 'norm' against which all forms of enslavement were measured, should be discarded. As slavery becomes more global, it becomes less obviously American. I propose that we might look at empires – another global institution as long-lasting and as widespread as slavery – as a better way to explore how societies managed human differences. Placing slavery in discussion with empires is not a perfect fit, but so often slavery was entrenched as a vital institution within empires, from ancient Greece, Rome and China, to the Ottomans and European seaborne empires in the early modern world, to American and West African proto-empires in the nineteenth century, and German and Soviet empires in the twentieth century. Consequently, examining slavery as intrinsic to various kinds of empire covers a great deal of the history of slavery and allows us to examine a particular area of interest which is usually central to empire – how does a polity manage difference in multi-ethnic environments?[10] Much can be gained from working out the interplay between imperial expansion and decline and slavery's role in unifying, as with the Ottomans and the Sokoto Caliphate, the identity of people in empire and, as in the Atlantic world, underpinning imperial prosperity.

The problem, however, with treating slavery as historically constructed and historically contingent as Miller suggests is that it lacks the conceptual rigour of sociological definitions of slavery. Miller's insistence that we study slavery as a function of history can be fuzzy around the edge. As Kostas Vlassopoulos notes, 'If slavery has an essence, but its historical manifestations differ substantially across time and space, how can we study slavery as a global phenomenon?'[11]

---

[8] Ibid., 31–4.

[9] Sebastian Conrad, *What Is Global History?* (Princeton: Princeton University Press, 2016), 55.

[10] Peter Fibiger Bang, 'Empire – A World History: Anatomy and Concept, Theory and Synthesis', in Peter Fibiger Bang, C. A. Bayly and Walter Scheidel, eds., *The Oxford World History of Empire: Vol. 1: The Imperial Experience* (Oxford: Oxford University Press, 2021), 12.

[11] Kostas Vlassopoulos, 'Does Slavery Have a History? The Consequences of a Global Approach', *Journal of Global Slavery* 1 (2016), 6.

How do we overcome this indeterminacy and provide some precision to our analysis? How can we deal with slavery as a massive global process while being attentive to the accretion of place-based knowledge about slavery in different places and times? In short, the study of global history in the twenty-first century is connected to a major historical problem – what we can call the global–local divide. Historians of slavery, like historians of globalisation generally, want to marry the global with the local so that we acknowledge the flows and movements of slavery on a global side without ignoring the diversity of processes and contexts that feed into these global flows and movements. Addressing this problem has led to a renewed enthusiasm for microhistories – studies that are explicitly not just about history on the small scale but about making local circumstances fit into larger patterns of historical change. Historians have become very interested in *jeux d'eschelles* or playing with scales of analysis, so that small-scale investigations can mix with medium-sized studies and with large kinds of analysis.[12] As Christian De Vito argues:

> Micro-spatial history seeks to bring power back to the centre of historical narratives, through the analysis of its concrete manifestations across space and in the configurations of social practices and networks. This is perhaps one area where the concept of scale might be useful: neither as a notion that describes allegedly existing 'sizes' or 'levels', nor as a tool to observe historical processes. Rather, as a social construction, scale can be studied to understand the ways in which historical actors think and produce 'vertical' binaries such as local/global, agency/structure and periphery/centre.[13]

Micro-spatial history might be the answer to making the history of slavery global while remaining attentive to local circumstances. In this Element I follow Anne Gerritsen and Christian De Vito's proposal that microhistory 'can provide the epistemological foundations for a renewed social history through its sensitivity to contextualization and historical distinctiveness through time and space' while 'spatial history can help microhistory to overcome its tendency to remain confined in geographically limited spaces and to conceptualise localities as self-sufficient units'.[14] De Vito's interpretation is complicated and depends upon an understanding of looking at a society from a local view with global perspectives.

---

[12] John-Paul A. Ghobrial, 'Many Stories and What They Tell Us: Early Modern Mobility between Microhistory and Global History', *Past & Present* 242 (2019), 243–80; Jan de Vries, 'Playing with Scales: The Global and the Micro, the Macro and the Nano', *Past & Present* 242 (2019), 23–36.

[13] Christian G. De Vito, 'History without Scales: The Micro-Spatial Perspective', *Past & Present* 242 (2019), 348–72.

[14] Christian G. De Vito and Anne Gerritsen, 'Micro-Spatial Histories of Global Labour: Towards a New Global History', in Christian G. De Vito and Anne Gerritsen, eds., *Micro-Spatial Histories of Global Labour* (New York: Palgrave Macmillan, 2018), 15.

The advantage of this micro-spatial approach is to deny a separation between a bird's-eye (global) view of slavery and a detailed analysis of its specific local features.

De Vito uses Miller's idea of slavery as a set of processes and practices insofar as 'it looks behind the concept of slavery and addresses the diverse practices by which men, women, and children are turned into slaves, it asks what slavery meant to different individuals and groups within specific localities; and it studies how and why the legal status and subjective perceptions of slavery changed across time'. 'From this perspective', De Vito concludes, 'we may say that micro-spatial history deconstructs universal concepts and reconstructs the histories, meanings and representations that are submerged within them'.[15] A particular advantage of a micro-spatial approach informed by Miller's historical strategies is that it gives a special place for understanding slave agency and resistance, as these are embedded in concrete historical practices.

This historical approach and close attention to how structures are not abstract but are 'constructed by social practices, located in connected individuals and groups, and embedded in specific social rules, legal systems, institutions and customs'[16] coincides with another major theme in the history of global slavery, which is to prioritise 'survivor' voices. In other words, scholars increasingly devote much attention to discovering how enslaved people themselves made sense of their predicament as enslaved people and how they construct narratives around the testimony they create and which become part of the historical record. Whether all enslaved people are 'survivors' if they come from ancient or medieval worlds where dependency was the status of almost everyone in society except a privileged few can be a matter of debate. But using techniques of historical excavation to ascertain how enslaved people thought and behaved, as best as we are able, produces, I argue, increasingly great rewards and helps us connect the local to the global. Paying more attention to the voices of the enslaved than we used to do in a historiography of slavery concerned more about structures than historical processes and practices helps us understand the variety of enslaved experiences and how those experiences were constructed in relation to particular historical circumstances. Ideally, it opens up the study of slavery to global experience, although in fact, as Section 3 hints at in its discussion of how enslaved testimony might be interrogated as highly compromised sources, the example of America as the norm from which slavery might be viewed is enhanced, given the ways in which slave narratives are a distinctly nineteenth-century American phenomenon. As Laura Murphy

---

[15] De Vito, 'History without Scales', 356. See also Courtney J. Campbell, 'Space, Place and Scale: Human Geography and Spatial History in Past and Present', *Past & Present* 239 (2018), 23–45.
[16] De Vito, 'History without Scales', 360.

argues, the nineteenth-century American slave narratives had such explanatory power that it is hard to transcend the powerful icon of the African in chains, which dominates such narratives, producing, for example, for contemporary survivors of slavery 'a crisis of illegibility' due to how the public learns from American slave narratives that slavery was permanently abolished in the nineteenth century.[17]

The following three sections outline the themes noted in this section in more detail, such as treating slavery as a set of historical practices and processes, paying less attention to nineteenth-century American slavery as the norm against which all slavery needs to be judged, using empire as a useful category of historical analysis within which to place the study of slavery and devoting close attention to the voices of the enslaved in shaping how we understand variegated but connected slave systems. This is a short Element. Thus, the ambition is not to be authoritative but to provoke thoughts and ideas which might help us understand global slavery better.

1 Models of Slavery

Slavery Today

As David Stefan Doddington and Enrico Del Lago note in their introduction to a stimulating set of essays on the historiography of slavery, 'slavery has existed almost everywhere around the globe where humans have laid roots and most human societies have, at one point or another, either practiced forms of slavery or faced enslavement themselves'.[18] That slavery is ubiquitous in history has never been widely contested. Indeed, it has often been thought of as essential to human development. The early twentieth-century poet and classicist A. E. Housman argued that 'civilization without slavery is impossible'.[19] Slavery remains, even after its formal abolition in every country in the world, a major global institution. In gross population terms, slavery has never been more widespread than it is today even if the percentage of enslaved people constitutes a much smaller percentage of the world's population, with 40.3 million slaves amounting to around 0.7–0.8 per cent of total population than it did in the global peak of

---

[17] Audrey Fisch, ed., *The Cambridge Companion to the African American Slave Narrative* (Cambridge: Cambridge University Press, 2007); Laura T. Murphy, *The New Slave Narrative: The Battle of Representations of Contemporary Slavery* (New York: Columbia University Press, 2019), 391.

[18] David Stefan Doddington and Enrico Del Lago, 'Writing the History of Slavery', in David Stefan Doddington and Enrico Del Lago, eds., *Writing the History of Slavery* (London: Bloomsbury Academic, 2022), 1. See also Damian Pargas and Juliane Schiel, *The Palgrave Handbook of Global Slavery through History* (Basingstoke: Palgrave Macmillan, 2023).

[19] Keith Bradley, 'Imagining Slavery in Roman Antiquity', in Doddington and Del Lago, *Writing the History of Slavery*, 307.

slavery around 1800 when 45 million chattel slaves amounted to 4.7 per cent of the world's population.[20]

The History of Writing about Slavery

Slavery is an institution and practice of world historical importance. The extent of recent scholarship on slavery can be seen in four monumental works. The first is the four-volume *Cambridge World History of Slavery*, which covers the history of slavery in almost all places in the world, except the Pacific save for a brief discussion of indentured servitude or 'blackbirding' in the late nineteenth century by Rosemarie Hoefte.[21] The second is Michael Zeuske's heroic single-volume guide to the historiography of slavery, a work notable for its emphasis on broad comparable themes and topics.[22] The third is the bestselling French compendium of fifty essays on aspects of global slavery, with special reference to 'situations', 'comparisons' and 'transformations'.[23] Finally, Damien Pargas and Juliane Schiel have compiled a large volume of thirty-two essays and five 'injections' (speculative essays on themes raised in sections of essays on global history). Each essay is based around three themes – how slaves entered slavery; their experiences while enslaved; and how people exited slavery, though not necessarily into freedom. They have deliberately limited the number of essays on Atlantic slavery to just four 'in order to help readers place Atlantic slavery – which was in many respects atypical and exceptional – within a wider global context and to allow more space for other case studies'.[24]

It was different in the recent past. The study of slavery as a world institution hardly existed in the nineteenth and the early twentieth centuries, except to a limited extent regarding ancient Greek and Roman slavery. The one remarkable exception was the extraordinary three-volume global history of slavery through-out the ancient world written by the Cuban polymath José Antonio Saco in the 1870s.[25] Equally remarkable, though mainly about the psychological effects of

---

[20] Andrea Nicholson, *Bearing Witness: Contemporary Slave Narratives and the Global Antislavery Movement* (Cambridge: Cambridge University Press, 2022), 2; David Eltis, 'Introduction', in David Eltis, Stanley L. Engerman, Seymour Drescher, and David Richardson, eds., *The Cambridge World History of Slavery: Vol. 4: AD1804–AD2016* (Cambridge: Cambridge University Press, 2017), 5.

[21] Rosemarie Hoefte, 'Indenture in the Long Nineteenth Century', in Eltis, *Cambridge World History of Slavery 4*, 623–4.

[22] Michael Zeuske, *Handbuch Geschichte der Sklaverei: Eine Globalgeshichte von den Anfongen bis zur Gegenwart*, 2nd ed. (Berlin: De Gruyter, 2019).

[23] Paulin Ismard, Benedetta Rossi and Cécile Vidal, eds., *Les Mondes de L'Esclavage: Une Historie Comparée* (Paris: Seul, 2021).

[24] Pargas and Schiel, *Palgrave Handbook of Global Slavery*, 10.

[25] José Antonio Saco, *Historia de la escavitud desde los tiempos más remotos hasta nuestros dias*, 3 vols. (Paris: Kugelmann, 1875).

slavery on enslaved Africans, was W. E. B. Du Bois' magisterial and lastingly influential meditation of 1903 on how racism and oppression created what Du Bois called 'double-consciousness'. Du Bois considered that Black Americans suffered from a conflicted self: 'an American, a Negro; two souls, two thoughts, two unreconciled strivings, two warring ideals in one dark body'.[26]

Saco and Du Bois were exceptions in a historical landscape largely indifferent to slavery, especially outside the Americas. As Miller notes, 'slavery around the world pulled off one of the more artful disappearing acts of the early twentieth century'. 'Slavery', he stated, 'was marginalised in public discourse and not yet embraced as a subject suitably remote for contemplation as history'.[27] Works on slavery in the 1930s and 1940s were rare, although they included two very influential works, by Caribbean scholars, on the Haitian Revolution, by C. L. R. James in 1938 and on how Britain profited from West Indian slavery, by Eric Williams in 1944.[28] It also included Frank Tannenbaum's 1946 polemical contrasting of a supposedly gentler slave system in Iberian New World colonies to a more brutal British American slave system.[29] Finally, the brilliant Brazilian sociologist, Gilberto Freyre, developed an interpretation of modern Brazil founded on a historical understanding of Brazil as a mestizo nation (though he used the word mulatto, which we probably would not use today) by substituting cultural diversity for biology and racial miscegenation.[30]

In general, historians saw a linear story that connected Graeco-Roman slavery to Atlantic slavery and to abolition and ignored slavery that existed outside these narrow boundaries. This historical indifference to slavery ended abruptly in the mid-twentieth century with studies of ancient and American slavery. In particular, the explosion of scholarship in the third quarter of the twentieth century on antebellum US slavery proved immensely influential in producing a model of what slavery is like, a model which has shaped until the last two decades most comparative studies of slavery and a kind of slavery against which every other kind of slavery is judged.[31] The deeply researched

---

[26] W. E. B. Du Bois, 'The Souls of Black Folk', in Nathan Huggins, ed., *W.B. Du Bois: Writings* (New York: Library of America, 1986), 364–5.

[27] Miller, *Problem of Slavery as History*, 37.

[28] C. L. R. James, *The Black Jacobins* (New York: Random House, 1938); Eric Williams, *Capitalism and Slavery* (Chapel Hill: University of North Carolina Press, 1944).

[29] Frank Tannenbaum, *Slave and Citizen* (New York: Vintage, 1946).

[30] Gilberto Freyre, *Casa-grande e Senzala* (Rio de Janeiro: Olympiio, 1933), trans. Samuel Putnam, *The Masters and the Slaves: A Study in the Development of Brazilian Civilization* (New York: Random House, 1946).

[31] Robert Fogel and Stanley Engerman, *Time on the Cross: The Economics of American Negro Slavery* (New York: Little, Brown, 1974); John W. Blassingame, *The Slave Community: Plantation Life in the Antebellum South* (New York: Oxford University Press, 1972); and Herbert G. Gutman, *The Black Family in Slavery and Freedom, 1750–1925* (New York: Vintage, 1976).

and theoretically ambitious doulotic studies of slavery by Eugene Genovese were especially influential. Being a Marxist, then a recovered Marxist, with a deep dislike of capitalism, Genovese stressed the paternalistic singularity of the antebellum slave system, although Genovese insisted that southern paternalism was one in which enslaved people exercised significant agency. Walter Johnson noted in 2001 that Genovese's *Roll, Jordan, Roll* has been 'the *locus classicus* for some of the most powerful and important ideas that have shaped the discussion of slavery for the last quarter century'.[32] It remains a model of scholarship, even while historians have modified its picture of a relatively harmonious slave community oriented around collectivist goals of communal advancement.[33]

The antebellum US South plays a disproportionate role in the historiography of slavery, connected to the outsized importance of the USA in global affairs and to the singular importance that Americans have customarily placed upon slavery and race, shaping American history. We can see its centrality in the enormous success of the Museum of Afro American History in Washington, DC, opened to great fanfare in 2016 by President Barack Obama, and in the prolonged controversy over *The New York Times'* Pulitzer Prize winning *1619 Project*, which argues for a redefinition of American history around the history of slavery rather than around freedom.[34] One need not belabour the point that the study of slavery in the US South is always the largest category of scholarship in the annual bibliographic supplements on slavery done for the journal *Slavery & Abolition*. In addition, the amount of primary material available to study antebellum US slavery, from plantation records to anti-slavery and pro-slavery polemics, to bestselling novels such as *Uncle Tom's Cabin* (1857), to congressional and state debates and to material culture and archaeological evidence, is appreciably greater than for any other place or time where slavery existed. Moreover, we have access to the individual voices of enslaved people in quantity and quality that is of a different league to what is found anywhere else in the archive of slavery.

---

[32] Eugene Genovese, *Roll, Jordan, Roll: The World the Slaves Made* (New York: Pantheon, 1974); Walter Johnson, 'A Nettlesome Classic Turns Twenty-Five', *Commonplace* 1.4 (July 2001). www.commonplace-archives,org/vol-01/no-4/reviews/Johnson.shtml.

[33] Jeff Forret, *Slave against Slave: Plantation Violence in the Old South* (Baton Rouge: Louisiana State University Press, 2015); Damian Pargas '"In the Fields of a Strange Land": Enslaved Newcomers and the Adjustment to Cotton Cultivation in the Antebellum South', *Slavery & Abolition* 34 (2013), 564–80; and Anthony E. Kaye, 'The Second Slavery: Modernity in the Nineteenth-Century South and the Atlantic World', *Journal of Southern History* 75 (2009), 627–50.

[34] Eliga Gould, Paul Mapp and Carla Gardina Pestana, eds., *Cambridge History of America and the World: Vol. 1: 1500–1820* (Cambridge: Cambridge University Press, 2021); Nikole Hannah-Jones, ed., *The 1619 Project: A New American Origin Story* (New York: W. H. Allen, 2021).

The idea that the plantations of the American South were paradigmatic and thus should form the principal source of comparison between slaveries over place and time is evidenced in the extraordinarily influential thesis by the twentieth-century Marxist-influenced historian of ancient Greece, Moses Finley. Finley distinguished between 'genuine' slave societies, each of which had to meet a series of more or less arbitrary measures that Finley outlined, and other societies that he described as 'societies with slaves', which in effect diminished the importance of slavery in these places as being epiphenomenal rather than foundational, or constitutive of social, political and economic relations.[35]

As Noel Lemski argues, 'Finley's model is vitiated by an unstated but clear assumption that the quintessential ideal type of purified slavery was found in the US South.' Finley also had problems with his model when his slave societies followed patterns different from those in the USA, as when Athenian slaves were more integrated into larger economic patterns than in the American South and when this economy was not composed of market-oriented plantations. Lemski notes that Finley usually compared ancient slavery to US slavery rather than to examples in the Caribbean and Brazil. He concludes that this usual comparison was problematic for such matters as slave resistance where 'in order to fit the comparative evidence to this pattern', Finley 'downplayed the significance of rebellion in other slaveholding systems'.[36]

Slave rebellion may have been infrequent in ancient Greece, as in the US South, but that was not true for Finley's other slave societies – ancient Rome, the Caribbean and Brazil. Elsa Goveia developed a model of enslavement for the eighteenth-century Leeward Islands which was remarkably similar to that of Finley though seemingly developed independently of Finley. Goveia, as a Caribbean specialist, put more emphasis on rebellion than did Finley. It does not appear, moreover, that Finley was aware of Goveia's work when he formulated his model. Goveia argued that by the end of the eighteenth century, slavery in the Leeward Islands was not just an economic organisation but was an institution around which the entire society was organised, socially and politically. She argued that slavery was so entrenched in the British controlled islands of the Lesser Antilles that it was indispensable for the maintenance of White planter order. She contended that the rulers of the island found it impossible to envision alternatives to slavery as a social and political organising principle

---

[35] Moses Finley, 'Slavery', in David L. Sills, ed., *International Encyclopedia of the Social Sciences* (New York: Macmillan, 1968), 308; Keith Hopkins, *Conquerors and Slaves: Sociological Studies in Roman History*, vol. 1 (Cambridge: Cambridge University Press, 1978).

[36] Noel Lemski, 'Ancient Slaveries and Modern Ideologies', in Lemski and Cameron, *What Is a Slave Society?* 115, 129.

even when slavery was starting to become unprofitable. Caribbean scholars have adopted, following Goveia rather than Finley, the concept of 'slave society', as an organising paradigm, as in fellow Caribbeanist Orlando Patterson's empirical studies on Jamaica. Why Goveia attracted less attention than Finley in developing this concept is unclear. Perhaps the limited number of works on Caribbean slavery and emancipation written before an efflorescence of scholarship on British Caribbean slavery from the early 1970s onwards confined her influence to a relatively small circle of Caribbean scholars.[37]

The comparative problems with the USA as a paradigm of slavery would be even greater if the US South was compared to several other societies that Lemski believes meet the qualifications for being a slave society, such as ancient Carthage and Sarmada, nineteenth-century Dahomey and the Sokoto Caliphate, the eighteenth-century Pacific Northwest, early modern Korea and nineteenth-century Eastern Arabia and the Persian Gulf.[38] A major problem, however, with taking antebellum southern slavery as the norm against which slavery elsewhere needs to be tested is that the 'peculiar institution', as it was known at the time was indeed peculiar among systems of global slavery. As Damian Pargas argues 'although the nineteenth-century US South has often served as a static proxy for systems of racial slavery in the modern era, this slaveholding society in fact developed out of a number of structural transformations that radically altered the nature of slavery and freedom in the Atlantic world'. Southern slavery, he notes, 'grew at an unprecedented rate, transforming half of the US into a "cotton kingdom" – with cotton production surging from 3,000 bales in 1790 to over 4 million bales in 1860 – and became characterized by a number of unique features, including a slave population that was almost entirely born in slavery; the development of a massive internal slave trade that wrought havoc on slave communities; the dominance of cotton plantation agriculture in the lives of most enslaved people; the curtailment of manumissions; and the rise of a continent-wide refugee crisis, as freedom seekers fled to parts of the continent where slavery had been abolished'. He concludes that it was different to other slave systems in the nineteenth-century Americas, which were showing signs that they were set on the path to destruction. The slave system in the American South was getting stronger every year, was expanding geographically, with a rapidly increasing enslaved population, and

---

[37] Elsa V. Goveia, *Slave Society in the British Leeward Islands in the Eighteenth-Century* (New Haven: Yale University Press, 1965); B. W. Higman, 'The Invention of Slave Society', in Brian L. Moore, B.W. Higman, Carl Campbell and Patrick Bryan, *Slavery, Freedom, and Gender: The Dynamics of Caribbean Society* (Kingston: University of West Indies Press, 2001), 57–76.

[38] Lemski and Cameron, *What Is a Slave Society?* 26–38, 313–36, 356–7.

contained an economic prognosis for continued wealth-making that meant that it would have likely continued if the USA had not decided, through civil war, to end it.[39]

In addition, antebellum southern slavery was based on an extreme form of racism in which people of African descent were second-class citizens at best.[40] Other slave systems had a racial component, but, apart from the British and French Caribbean, no other society in which slavery existed was so reliant on racial definitions in order to justify people being held against their will. Not all Blacks in the US South were enslaved, though free Blacks were increasingly an anomaly that Whites wished would disappear with rates of manumission declining over the nineteenth century. From the middle of the eighteenth century, virtually no Whites were coerced workers and there were few indigenous slaves in North America, both categories of which were extensive within settler as well as indigenous polities in the seventeenth century.[41] American southern slavery was a social and political system predicated upon White supremacy and the natural inferiority and subordination of Black people. White Americans, moreover, believed in an extremely radical definition of race, where anyone with even the smallest amount of African inheritance – the notorious 'one-drop' rule – was defined as Black and thus subject to hard race laws, even if not enslaved.[42] The persistence in the American South of a pernicious racism in support of a legally and politically protected White supremacy meant that emancipation did not lead to formerly enslaved people becoming integrated, except briefly and incompletely, into southern politics and society as citizens with rights equal to those of White people until well into the twentieth century.[43] It also meant that race and slavery went together. As Paul Gilroy notes, 'It is hardly surprising that if it is perceived to be relevant at all, the history of slavery is somehow assigned to

---

[39] Damian Alan Pargas, 'Slavery in the US South', in Pargas and Schiel, *Palgrave Handbook of Global Slavery*, 441–58. See also Ira Berlin, *Generations of Captivity: A History of African-American Slaves* (Cambridge, MA: Harvard University Press, 2003), 159–244; and Walter Johnson, *River of Dark Dreams: Slavery and Empire in the Cotton Kingdom* (Cambridge, MA: Harvard University Press, 2017).

[40] Jacqueline Jones, *A Dreadful Deceit: The Myth of Race from the Colonial Era to Obama's America* (New York: Basic Books, 2017) and Ibram Kendi, *Stamped from the Beginning: The Definitive History of Racial Idea in America* (New York: Nation Books, 2016).

[41] Andrés Reséndez, *The Other Slavery: The Uncovered Story of Indian Enslavement in America* (New York: Mariner Books, 2017).

[42] Berlin, *Generations of Captivity,* 119–23, 135–50, 159–244; Sue Peabody and Keila Grinberg, 'Free Soil: The Generation and Circulation of an Atlantic Legal Principle', *Slavery & Abolition* 32 (2011), 331–9.

[43] Douglas Blackmon, *Slavery by Another Name: The Re-enslavement of African Americans from the Civil War to World War Two* (New York: Anchor Books, 2008).

blacks. It becomes part of our special property rather than a part of the ethical and intellectual heritage of the West as a whole.'[44]

Finally, antebellum America was deeply divided over slavery, with much of the USA firmly opposed to slavery on philosophical and economic grounds and a smaller but not inconsiderable section of White Americans convinced that slavery was the central support of a well-ordered, hierarchical and patriarchal social order.[45] Few slave owners in history before the start of British and American abolitionism in the late eighteenth century ever had to worry about opposition to their ownership of people. And in no other society was slavery ended with a catastrophic long-term conflict in which not only were slave-holders comprehensively defeated but were given no compensation for their enslaved property, a singular event in the emancipation process.[46] As always, however, the end of slavery was not accompanied by any money or land being distributed to enslaved people as recognition for their mistreatment and exploit-ation under slavery. The development of a racialised system of African slavery in the New World designed for the capitalist production of the Americas was unusual in its scope, intensity and consequences. As Damian Pargas notes, the American South developed out of a number of major structural transformations where there was both an unprecedented expansion of Black freedom and an equally unprecedented expansion of slavery.[47]

Antebellum American slavery was harsh, but the torments enslaved people faced were as much psychological as physical. Enslaved people had multiple ways of asserting their self against enslaver attempts to obliterate their sense of individual self-worth, but they suffered greatly from harsh physical and psy-chological pressures. The enslavers' paternalistic interest in their slaves as members of a supposed 'family', which so impressed Eugene Genovese was mostly a farce. As Walter Johnson has argued, southern White paternalism was more a desperate alibi against abolitionist attacks than a genuine ideology.[48] Owners' lack of concern about their enslaved 'family' and their willingness to sell them without consideration for enslaved people's actual families

---

[44] Paul Gilroy, *The Black Atlantic: Modernity and Double Consciousness* (Cambridge, MA: Harvard University Press, 1993), 49.

[45] Manisha Sinha, *The Slave's Cause: A History of Abolition* (New Haven: Yale University Press, 2017); David Brion Davis, *The Problem of Slavery in the Age of Revolutions* (Ithaca: Cornell University Press, 1975); Richard M. Blackett, *The Captive's Quest for Freedom: Fugitive Slaves, the 1850 Fugitive Slave Law, and the Politics of Slavery* (New York: Cambridge University Press, 2018).

[46] Frédérique Beauvois, *Between Blood and Gold: The Debates over Compensation in the Americas* (Oxford: Berghan Books, 2017).

[47] Pargas, 'Slavery in the US South', 441–58.

[48] Walter Johnson, *Soul by Soul: Life inside the Antebellum Slave Market* (Cambridge, MA: Harvard University Press, 1999).

demonstrated how little they cared for Blacks and how deeply they despised them. Antebellum southern slavery was thus distinctive, exhibiting characteristics that made it exceptional rather than normative. Thus, an interesting question remains: if nineteenth-century American slavery was exceptional and not the model by which to compare slavery in other times and places, what do we replace this model with?

Existing Models

Conceptual models of slavery are relatively limited in number and impact. Moreover, scholars are increasingly resistant to following the models that exist, as the amount of research into global slavery has less validated than complicated wide-ranging comparative studies. An emphasis on archival empirical work and a continuing insistence that more research with often very recalcitrant sources after needed makes authors reluctant to use grand theories that categorise enslavement are especially noticeable in the survey of medieval enslavement in Volume 2 of the *Cambridge World History of Slavery*.[49] We are in a moment of flux in how we think about slavery, on the cusp of foundational change but without a clear appreciation of how we should approach the subject, especially as the primacy of the antebellum US slave system as 'normative' falters. The fundamental shifts in our understanding of slavery have not yet occurred. Increasingly, as Joseph Miller has argued, our approach to global slavery is more influenced by history than by sociology.[50] The problem with this historical approach, however, is that it is so vague and diffuse as to make comparisons across space and time difficult: if context is everything then each slave system becomes *sui generis*. The implication we can draw is that scholars are more convinced about what they are against than what they are in favour of.

The theory of slavery that meets with the most disfavour is that advanced by Karl Marx and his followers, in which slavery is a stage process from feudalism to slavery to capitalism in Western Europe and European offshoots in the New World. Scholars of slavery in late antiquity doubt that this period fitted Marxist ideas of a time of transition during which systems of tied tenant labour displaced the slave villa as the dominant form of economic exploitation. They consider that this misreads the extent to which slavery in late antiquity resembled slavery in ancient Rome.[51] Medievalists are especially disinclined to follow Marxist ideas. For Michal Biran, for example, Marxist theories have 'marred' previous surveys of slavery in the Mongol Empire, while for Ali Anooshahr, writing

---

[49] Trevor Burnard, 'A Global History of Slavery in the Medieval Millennium', *Slavery & Abolition* 43 (2022), 820.

[50] Miller, *Problem of Slavery as History*, 24–5.

[51] Kyle Harper, 'The Transformation of Roman Slavery: An Economic Myth?' *Antiquité tardive* 20 (2012), 165–72.

about medieval North India, Marxism is 'baggage' from which scholars need to be 'unburdened'.[52] For historians of later periods, where Marxist analyses fall down is in Marx's belief that slavery was not capitalist, making chattel slavery incompatible with a capitalist system that depended upon consumers and skilled workers responding to incentives. And Marxist analyses work poorly for non-Western societies because, as Anthony Reid notes:

> Feudalism and capitalism have already needed so much subdivision and nuance to make sense outside medieval Europe – and even within it – that they hardly survive as useful global categories.[53]

There is, however, some acceptance of the Marxist position that any ruling class will impose slavery on others if it is allowed to do so and an increasing insistence by scholars attached to the new History of Capitalism movement that slavery was fundamental to imperialism and that imperialism was central to the development of capitalism.[54]

Where scholars diverge from Marx is how he saw slavery as not decisive to the capitalist mode of production as it did not involve wage labour. Even the most impressive Marxist analysis of slavery modifies Marx in this respect. Robin Blackburn's magisterial panoramic survey of the making of New World slavery from 1492 to 1800 argues in support of Marx's contention that colonialism in the Americas, including slavery, facilitated what Marx called 'primitive accumulation', which eventually ended up in industrial capitalism. Blackburn argues that 'the colonial and Atlantic regime of extended primitive accumulation allowed metropolitan accumulation to break out of its agrarian and national limits and discover an industrial and global destiny'. Nevertheless, Blackburn qualifies Marx not only in seeing slavery as capitalist and modern from the start but also in noting that the forms of colonial depredation that Marx noted 'did not promote truly capitalist accumulation because their profits were seized by rulers who spent them on their own aggrandizement, or adventurers who aspired to become landed aristocrats'. As Richard Pares quipped in regard to Eric Williams' assertion that slavery fuelled British industrialisation, slave profits led to more Fonthills (a country house belonging to the slaveholding Beckford family) than factories.[55]

---

[52] Michael Biran, 'Forced Migrations and Slavery in the Mongol Empire (1206–1328)'; and Ali Annooshahr, 'Military Slavery in Medieval North India', in Craig Perry, David Eltis, Stanley L. Engerman and David Richardson, *Cambridge World History of Slavery 2*, 82, 362.

[53] Anthony Reid, '"Slavery So Gentle": A Fluid Spectrum of Southeast Asian Conditions of Bondage', in Lemski and Cameron, *What Is a Slave Society?* 424.

[54] Sven Beckert, *Empire of Cotton: A New History of Global Capitalism* (New York: Penguin, 2014).

[55] Robin Blackburn, *The Making of New World Slavery: From the Baroque to the Modern, 1492–1800* (London: Verso, 1997), 514–15; Richard Pares, 'Merchants and Planters', *Economic History Review* suppl. 4 (1960), 50.

Orlando Patterson's masterpiece from 1982 is the book that continues to attract most attention among specialists of slavery, being easily the most cited model in comparative global studies.[56] He formulated a universally valid definition of the basic constitutive elements of slavery. Patterson's vast erudition, analytical rigour and bold synthesis of wide-ranging data have evoked widespread admiration, while his explanation of how enslaved people entered slavery either 'intrusively' (slaves sourced from outside the enslaving society) or 'extrusively' (slaves sourced from within a society as a result of violating social, criminal or economic norms) continues to be influential. But his most fiercely argued claim, that slavery was for individuals enmeshed in it a kind of 'social death', psychologically akin to real death, whereby slaves were stripped of all sense of belonging to a polity, community or family, has proved more controversial and is increasingly less accepted.[57]

In practice, scholars have argued, enslaved people were not so affected by natal alienation as to become non-persons. They still displayed agency and sometimes became integrated to the point of becoming community leaders, as with the Mamluks in Egypt.[58] Patterson's theory of social death is criticised as too rigid and at the same time too vague and overly influenced by his grounding in the extreme slave system of eighteenth-century Jamaica. Frederick Cooper argues that not only does Patterson's model ignore slave agency, it is too focused on slaveholders' ideas of how slavery ought to work rather than about how the system actually played out in practice.[59] Joel Quirk believes that Patterson is unclear about whether slavery is a liminal state of social death or the permanent and violent domination of one person over someone depicted as socially dead. It makes, according to critics, slavery as much a state of mind as a relationship based on property ownership and upon forced labour.[60] Patterson's model, nevertheless, remains one to engage with, as it takes seriously the cultural isolation of the enslaved.[61]

---

[56] Orlando Patterson, *Slavery and Social Death: A Comparative Study* (Cambridge: Harvard University Press, 1982).

[57] Vincent Brown, 'Social Death and Political Life in the Study of Slavery', *American Historical Review* 114 (2009), 1231–49; Bodel and Scheidel, *On Human Bondage*.

[58] Stephan Conermann, 'Slavery in the Mamluk Sultanate', in Craig Perry, David Eltis, Stanley L. Engerman and David Richardson, *Cambridge World History of Slavery 2*, 383–405.

[59] Frederick Cooper, *Colonialism in Question: Theory, Knowledge, History* (Berkeley: University of California Press, 2005), 17.

[60] Lewis, 'Orlando Patterson, Property and Ancient Slavery'; Joel Quirk, 'The Anti-Slavery Project: Linking the Historical and Contemporary', *Human Rights Quarterly* 28 (2006): 569. For a riposte, see Orlando Patterson and Xiaolin Zhuo, 'Modern Trafficking, Slavery and Other Forms of Servitude', *Annual Review of Sociology* 44 (2018), 410.

[61] Nicholas T. Rinehart, 'The Man That Was a Thing: Reconsidering Human Commodification', *Journal of Social History* 50 (2016), 1–23.

Moses Finley's notion of a division between 'slave societies', societies in which a considerable percentage of the population (at least 20 per cent) were enslaved and where slavery was an indispensable feature of society and especially the economy, and 'societies with slaves', where slavery was present but where the enslaved were not large enough in numbers and importance to indelibly shape social and economic patterns is perhaps as influential as Patterson's model has been. In this schema, only five societies, two in the ancient world and three in the New World, were 'genuine' slave societies. This model has been increasingly questioned as we develop more research on global slavery. Anthony Reid notes that the concept of 'slave society' was more of a provocation than a useful global category of analysis and that it is better to see slavery 'as one among many systems of servile labor exploitation and not necessarily the most cruel and inhumane'. Where it has been seen as 'useful' is as shorthand to clarify points historians might look at in understanding an enslaving society. Otherwise, the attitude taken has been rather dismissive, accepted only because it is familiar and simple to understand, and when it does not work, it is not invalidated because historians seldom expect models to work in all places and at all times.[62]

In general, the 'slave societies' concept has eroded in acceptability as it has expanded past Finley's original and restrictive definition. It seems too Eurocentric and ethnocentric. While Finley was very precise in what constituted a slave society, the qualifications – a large percentage of the population being enslaved and heavily involved in the economy – are arbitrary and predetermining. In particular, the model undermines the harshness of the lived experience of being enslaved in 'societies with slaves', like medieval China or early modern New England. Relatively few people were enslaved in such societies, but that does not mean that they had easy lives. Lemski outlines many of the faults in the Finley model – its oversimplification of complicated social relations; its lack of precision in accounting for differences between 'slave societies', let alone between all societies with slaves; its reliance on nineteenth-century America as a model. Lemski ends by claiming that 'Finley's model has had its time' and that what we need now are historically rather than sociologically influenced comparative case studies of slavery. 'The Finleyan model', he concludes, 'for all that it brought the dialogue forward in the mid-twentieth century, is now preventing it from making further progress'.[63]

Noel Lemski and Catherine M. Cameron conclude that while scholars invested in the study of Western Europe and colonial offshoots of Europe still find value in Finley's model, scholars studying non-western societies and modern slavery are less comfortable with the construct, even when many of

---

[62] Reid, '"Slavery So Gentle"', 427; Ehud R. Toledano, 'Ottoman and Islamic Societies; Were They "Slave Societies"?' in Lemski and Cameron, *What Is a Slave Society?* 362–3.

[63] Lemski, 'Framing the Question', 123–4, 147.

the societies they study could be considered slave societies.[64] One reason for this reluctance to embrace Finley's model is the explicit nods to the nineteenth-century American South being typical or 'normative'. Moreover, the concept of 'slave societies' works less well in places which are not focused much around capitalist market exchange. And certainly 'slave societies' were less remarkable and more variegated than Finley suggested. If we concentrate less on rigid sociological models in the manner of Finley and think of slavery as a set of practices and processes and historical strategies, we see fewer similarities than differences among slave societies. Each slave society, or society with slaves, Lemski and Cameron suggest, 'displays its own peculiarities, dictated by a set of variables unique to a given culture, and all arise from both economic and cultural tendencies that favour the intensification of slaveholding in environments that devalue the humanity of some group or class to the point that fellow people can be treated as mere chattels'.[65]

Thus, the existing models of slavery are proving ever less satisfactory. The deficiencies in existing models have led to a spike in new overarching theories, but none have really been taken up by historians. The three most promising models have been Dale Tomich and Michael Zeuske's model of 'second slavery', though this only refers to slavery in the nineteenth century, Jeff Fynn-Paul's conception of 'slaving zones', in which some places allowed the enslavement of insiders while others did not and which seems to work better for the medieval Mediterranean than for other places and Noel Lemski's suggestion of 'intensification', which is mostly a modification of Finley's 'slave society' model so that it avoids 'facile bipartite distinctions and simple division into opposing categories'.[66] Historians' lack of enthusiasm for new modes may arise from the nature of history as a discipline: historians are reluctant to embrace comprehensive models wholeheartedly as it violates the induction-driven and empirically and historically contingent principles which drive the historians' craft.[67]

Conclusion

When we consider the greatly expanded study of slavery in recent decades, three developments stand out. First, there has been a dramatic change in temporal and spatial focus so that slavery is written about as a genuinely global

---

[64] Lemski and Cameron, 'Introduction', 12. [65] Ibid., 14.

[66] Dale Tomich and Michael Zeuske, 'Introduction, the Second Slavery: Mass Slavery, World-Economy, and Comparative Microhistories', *Review (Fernand Braudel Center)* 31 (2008), 91–100; Jeff Fynn-Paul and Damian Alan Pargas, eds., *Slaving Zones, Cultural Identities, Ideologies, Institutions in the Evolution of Global Slavery* (Leiden: Brill, 2018); Lemski, 'Framing the Question', 54.

[67] Toledano, 'Ottoman and Islamic Societies', 361; Miller, *Problem of Slavery as History*, 24–9.

phenomenon.[68] Second, scholars have been less keen to see slavery in sociological terms as an implicitly static institution to adopting an approach that is more closely informed by historical perspectives. The past is contextualised in order to suggest the meanings and intentions of human actions that condition how forms of slavery develop rather than the past being de-contextualised as is common in sociology so that specific events and periods can be fitted into pre-existing models.[69] Third, historians are searching for new historically informed models, with only some degree of success, within which to place the varied and variable practices of slavery found in global history, meaning that well-established analytical models, such as Orlando Patterson's concept of social death and Moses Finley's (and Elsa Goveia's) separation of slavery into 'genuine' slave societies and less genuine societies that had slaves but where slavery was not institutionally and culturally dominant, are less persuasive than before. All of these changes are an almost inevitable consequence of the rise of a global slavery which is not coterminous with antebellum US slavery as the 'norm' against which all other kinds of slavery are compared. This approach has greatly expanded knowledge but has not perhaps increased clarity.

2 New Ways of Writing the History of Slavery

Introduction

If old ways of writing the history of slavery do not cover the variety of global slavery and if slavery in nineteenth-century America is more peculiar than normative, what models can we use to replace the discarded ones? Perhaps a historically inflected use of Atlantic history and even more a concentration on how empire-shaped patterns of slavery in many places over long periods of time might work better. That presumption is one that this section will test.

Damian Pargas has bravely attempted to isolate three interrelated themes in the current scholarship on slavery. First, he notes that slavery is at the extreme end of a broad spectrum – or continuum – of unfree and dependent conditions. His emphasis on dependency reflects the assumptions that undergird the study of slavery at the well-funded and increasingly influential Bonn Centre for Dependency and Slavery Studies (BCDSS). It is argued by BCDSS that slavery should be seen as an extreme case of asymmetrical dependency, defining asymmetrical dependence as 'the ability of one actor to control the actions and the access to resources of another, supported by an institutional background whereby the dependent actor cannot change their situation by either going away

---

[68] Damian Alan Pargas, 'Slavery as a Global and Globalizing Phenomenon: An Editorial Note', *Journal of Global Slavery* 1 (2016), 1–4.

[69] Miller, *Problem of Slavery as History*, 24–5.

(exit) or by articulating protest'. They have a particular, if ill-defined, animus at what they consider is one of the underlying assumptions in American slavery scholarship which is the binary opposition of slavery and freedom; wanting to replace this binary with the more capacious concept of dependency which they argue encompasses all diverse forms that human bondage and coercion have taken over time. To a large extent, this resistance to discourses about freedom results from how the BCDSS prioritises the work of premodern and non-western societies.[70]

The basis of BCDSS' asymmetrical dependency theory is sociological,[71] but it has a close attachment to historical approaches to slavery, being very deferential to Joseph Miller's argument about slaving as a historical strategy. It advocates that studies of slavery should follow the assumptions of micro-spatial history, an approach to history which combines social history's sensitivity to context and historical distinctiveness alongside an attention to historical geography so that 'spatial history can help micro-history overcome its tendency to remain confined in geographically limited spaces and to conceptualise localities as self-sufficient units'.[72] They suggest that the study of slavery might best be studied within a microhistorical approach that emphasises 'the centrality of historical agents, their practices and their strategies'.[73]

Second, Pargas comments that slavery is no longer depicted solely as a labour system and as having developed as a means of overcoming labour shortages in profit-seeking economic activities. The famous exposition of this view was made in 1900 by H. J. Nieboer and was refined in 1970 by the economist Evsey Domar, the latter arguing that 'free land, free persons and non-working landowners were mutually incompatible'. Only two of these elements, Nieboer and Domar argued, could exist at once, explaining the rise of serfdom in medieval Europe and slavery in Atlantic America. Orlando Patterson demolished much of the theoretical underpinnings of the Nieboer–Domar thesis in 1977, arguing that slavery encompassed more than just a relation to labour. Slavery, Patterson suggested, went beyond work and labour into such matters as power, prestige, privilege and sexual exploitation.[74]

---

[70] 'BCDSS Research Objectives', www.dependency.uni-bonn.de/en/our-research; David Eltis and Stanley L. Engerman, 'Dependence, Servility, and Coerced Labor in Time and Space', in David Eltis and Stanley L. Engerman, eds., *The Cambridge World History of Slavery: Vol. 3: AD 1420–AD 1804* (Cambridge: Cambridge University Press, 2011), 1–24.

[71] James S. Coleman, *Foundations of Social Theory* (Cambridge, MA: Harvard University Press, 1990); Albert O. Hirschman, *Exit, Voice, and Loyalty: Responses to Decline in Firms, Organizations, and States* (Cambridge, MA: Harvard University Press, 1970).

[72] De Vito and Gerritsen, 'Micro-Spatial Histories of Global Labour', 15.

[73] De Vito, 'History without Scales', 349, 351.

[74] Evsey D. Domar, 'The Causes of Slavery or Serfdom: A Hypothesis', *Journal of Economic History* 30 (1970), 18–32; Christian De Vito, Juliane Schiel, and Matthias van Rossum, 'From

Gender, for example, is increasingly important as a factor conditioning entry into and the experience of being enslaved. The modal slave is depicted more frequently than in the past as female rather than male, reflecting the extent to which slavery was about the exploitation of the reproductive as well as the productive capacities of women. Increased attention to gender has made gender historians aware that gender history and global history can be beneficial to each other, rather than, as Sebastian Conrad has argued, inherently opposed.[75] Diana Paton makes a powerful case for gender as decisive in shaping slavery. She deals with the area in which she has experience – Atlantic slavery – but suggests that her argument about the centrality of enslaved women's reproductive labour under plantation slavery might be applied to earlier periods of slavery. She insists that the subjugation of enslaved women was fundamental to Atlantic slave systems. 'What these systems shared', she argues, was organisations of gender and marriage which 'rendered white male sexual entitlement and legitimated sexual violence against enslaved women while ensuring that consolidated wealth remained in the hands of slave-owning families'. It was through patriarchal principles of inheritance and the heritability of status that we can understand gendered power relations and how, when women did not thrive demographically as in the Caribbean, that affected slave owners' capital accumulation as they did not get the benefit of additional and thus free labourers acquired through demographic increase.[76]

Finally, Pargas suggests that Orlando Patterson's influential assumption that our awareness of freedom was dependent on human experiences with slavery is being reassessed.[77] Historians are less convinced than they were that such a binary exists and have relied on enslaved voices to outline that enslaved people were not always seeking freedom when they acted as they did. Patterson, of course, recognised that definitions of freedom were a conceptual muddle, but his binary association of freedom with slavery is a model still used by scholars of Atlantic and American slavery.

Atlantic Slavery as a Model

These themes are sensible and are justified by Pargas' wide reading in the field and institutional prominence as the editor of an important journal on global slavery and his influence within European circles of slavery scholarship.

Bondage to Precariousness: New Perspectives on Labor and Social History', *Journal of Social History* 54 (2020), 1–19.
[75] Conrad, *What Is Global History?* 11–12.
[76] Diana Paton, 'Gender History, Global History, and Atlantic Slavery: On Racial Capitalism and Social Reproduction', *American Historical Review* 127 (2022), 741.
[77] Orlando Patterson, *Freedom in the Making of Western Culture* (New York: Basic Books, 1991).

I would add to his analysis an appreciation of how slavery is embedded within empires, which is the main theme of this section. That slavery was so often part of empires has led to antebellum American slavery being downplayed and slavery in the European empires of the early modern Atlantic world being highlighted. One hesitates to replace one stereotype for another, but one could argue that the modal slave in slavery studies is not the native born Christian enslaved person picking cotton in the antebellum South but an African-born slave transported in the horrific Middle Passage in the eighteenth century and set to work as a plantation slave growing sugar in the hell-holes of colonial Jamaica or Saint-Domingue.[78] The themes that are especially interesting to contemporary scholars of slavery are exemplified in the histories of these places, such as global migration, the relation of slavery to the rise of Europe vis-à-vis Asia through slavery's connections to capitalism and the importance of violence within the slave system.

The eighteenth-century Caribbean plantation was a remarkable wealth-generating machine and a monstrous invention of degradation. It produced sugar to satisfy Europe's sweet tooth, but it was a malign institution for the workers enmeshed in its coils. Yet slavery in plantation America was massively important in shaping the modern world. As Abbé Raynal, the eighteenth-century French philosophe, opined:

> the labours of the colonists settled in these long-scorned islands are the sole basis of the African trade, extend the fisheries and cultivation of North America, provide advantageous outlets for the manufacture of Asia, double perhaps triple the activity of the whole of Europe. They can be regarded as the principal cause of the rapid movement which stirs the universe.[79]

Barbara Solow notes: 'It was slavery that made the empty lands of the western hemisphere valuable producers of commodities and valuable markets for Europe and North America. What moved in the Atlantic in these centuries was predominantly slaves, the output of slaves, the inputs of slave societies, and the goods and services purchased with the earnings on slave products.'[80]

Of course, moving the centre of slavery earlier in time and closer to Europe and with a much stronger emphasis on extreme violence and displacement has

---

[78] I am conscious that this is my area of expertise but I note that two of the most highly regarded recent books on slavery have focused on slave revolts in the mid-eighteenth-century Caribbean. Vincent Brown, *Tacky's Revolt: The Story of an Atlantic Slave War* (Cambridge, MA: Harvard University Press, 2020) and Marjoleine Kars, *Blood on the River: A Chronicle of Mutiny and Freedom on the Wild Coast* (New York: New Press, 2020).

[79] Cited in Michael Duffy, *Soldiers, Sugar, and Seapower: The British Expedition to the West Indies and the War with Revolutionary France* (Oxford: Clarendon Press, 1987), 6.

[80] Barbara Solow, 'Slavery and Colonization', in Barbara Solow, ed., *Slavery and the Rise of the Atlantic System* (Cambridge: Cambridge University Press, 1991), 21–42.

its own problems. As Karen Bravo and Joel Quirk complain, in regard to modern slavery, having mid-eighteenth-century Atlantic slavery as the standard for what slavery is diminishes other forms of slavery than transatlantic slavery, which is a form of enslavement generally located at an exceptional position at the apex of a hierarchical scale of exploitation, vulnerability and coercion.[81] Greater attention to global slavery, however, has led to a more nuanced appreciation of slavery as a global practice and a globalising phenomenon.[82] Kostas Vlassopoulus emphasises how slavery needs to be placed within the context of it being a practice by arguing that 'we need to set aside the essentialist understanding of slavery and the ahistorical typology of slave societies and societies with slaves in favour of an understanding of slavery as a temporally – and spatially – changing outcome of the entanglement of various processes.'[83] Paulin Ismard supports such claims in insisting that comparative history has to pay attention to the historical contexts that shaped different slave systems, while Stefan Hanß and Juliane Schiel note that placing slavery as a historical practice within what they call 'the history of the everyday' focuses attention on 'how "lordship" or "rule" were relational categories that were not exercised without questioning but were negotiated in concrete situations through specific practices and discourses'.[84] Such an approach stresses contingency and sees slavery as open-ended and variable with very different experiences for the enslaved depending on where and when they were enslaved.

Empire and Slavery

The following section is not an attempt to add another model to the mix but to suggest that attention to one historically contingent but long-lasting and globally extensive institution – empire – can illuminate some aspects of another long-lasting and historically contingent institution – slavery. The move towards the study of slavery as a global institution has increasingly connected the study of slavery to the history of empires. Slavery, of course, is not confined to empires, but it is often associated with imperial expansion and the nature of imperialism, especially to the idea, advanced by Jane Burbank and Frederick Cooper, that empires were political entities that managed to incorporate diverse

---

[81] Karen Bravo, 'Exploring the Analogy between Modern Trafficking in Humans and the Transatlantic Slave Trade', *Buffalo International Law Journal* 25 (2007), 207–21; Joel Quirk, *The Antislavery Project: From the Slave Trade to Human Trafficking* (Philadelphia: University of Pennsylvania Press, 2011).

[82] Miller, *Problem of Slavery as History*, 9.   [83] Vlassopoulus, 'Does Slavery Have a History?'

[84] Paulin Ismard, 'Writing the History of Slavery: Between Comparison and Global History', *Annales: Histoire, Sciences Sociale* (English ed.), 72 (2017), 7–40; Stefan Hanß and Juliane Schiel, eds., *Mediterranean Slavery Revisited (500–1800)/Neue Perspektiven Auf Mediterrane Sklarei* (Zurich, Chronos Verlag, 2014), 17–20.

populations while reproducing distinctions and hierarchy. In particular, empires tend to exhibit a tension between wanting to celebrate homogeneity (though this impulse towards political and cultural homogeneity is more characteristic of nation states than empires)[85] and acknowledging the reality of social heterogeneity. Burbank and Cooper argue that how rulers governed unlike people and how the exercise of imperial power revolved to a large degree around what they call the 'politics of difference' are central to the study of imperialism. The methods used might be different (Burbank and Cooper counterpose the Roman and Mongol empires as adopting opposing governing strategies about including and excluding outsiders), but confronting the difference was central to imperial missions.[86] Another way of putting this is that empires depended on structures of marginality whereby politically powerful people overcame their own 'outsiderdom' to most people in diverse empires through using slavery to supplement their rule, usually demeaning those that were enslaved as suitable for enslavement due to religion, race or other kinds of difference that marked them out as being barbaric.[87]

The resurgence of interest in empire in recent decades has accompanied an increased interest in global slavery. Empire used to be thought of as old-fashioned, and its study had limited utility. In the 1980s, imperial historian D. K. Fieldhouse felt that imperial history had fallen into such disrepute that it might be 'condemned to share the midden of discredited academic subjects with, say, astrology or phrenology'.[88] Fieldhouse's pessimism was misplaced. Empire has become a frequent object of historical attention, partly because the twenty-first century events, from the invasion of Iraq in 2004 to the US and British occupation of Afghanistan to the 2022 war in Ukraine, are imperial projects and because the study of imperialism illuminates major historical questions, in particular the nature and exercise of power. After all, the etymological derivation of 'empire' is from the Latin word *imperium* which signifies power and the authority to command. It corresponds to similar words in non-European languages, such as *tianxin* in Mandarin, deriving from the claim of the first Chinese emperor in 221 BCE to have 'united all under heaven'.[89] Paul Kramer notes the advantages of an imperial perspective as being threefold: the way power resides in and operates through long-distance connections; the

---

[85] Siniša Malešević, 'Empires and Nation-States: Beyond the Dichotomy', *Thesis Eleven* 139 (2017), 3–10.

[86] Jane Burbank and Frederick Cooper, *Empires in World History: Power and the Politics of Difference* (Princeton: Princeton University Press, 2010).

[87] Miller, *Problem of Slavery as History*, 51–6.

[88] D. K. Fieldhouse, 'Can Humpty-Dumpty Be Put Together Again? Imperial History in the 1980s', *Journal of Imperial and Commonwealth History* 12 (1984), 9–23.

[89] Fibiger Bang, 'Empire – A World History', 12.

mutual and uneven transformation of societies through these connections; comparisons between large-scale systems of power and their histories.[90] Krisnan Kumar explains that 'empires, for all their faults, show us another way, a way of managing diversity and differences that are now the inescapable fate of practically all so-called nation-states'. 'That by itself', he argues, 'seems sufficient grounds for continuing to study them, and to reflect on what they might be able to teach us'. The study of empires engages current beliefs in multiculturalism, diasporas, migrations and multinationalism and is a prism through which the 'pressing problems of the contemporary world and even the birth pangs of a new world order' can be addressed.[91]

The study of empire has advantages for understanding global slavery through its explicit emphasis on power and because empires have a history almost as long as that of slavery itself. The experience of empire extends back to the third millennium BCE and spans across the globe. It is thus highly suitable for world history surveys and for comparative studies that cross traditional chronological periods and established geographical boundaries. Empires are composite, layered and structured around hierarchies and communities with a dominant power, multiple structures of power and heterogeneous, usually polyethnic, populations. Stephen Howe's succinct introduction to imperial studies states that 'a kind of basic, consensus definition would be that an empire is a large political body which rules over territory outside its original borders. It has a central power or core territory – whose inhabitants usually continue to form the dominant ethnic or natural group in the entire system- and an extensive periphery of dominated areas'.[92] Empires, as sociologist Garry Runciman argues, were 'a distinctive type of social formation' in which people inside empires were either absorbed 'to the point that they become fellow-members of the central society' or disengaged 'from them to the point that they became confederates rather than subjects'. Because empire 'endures in a convenient state between annexation and mere alliance', slavery was very often present.[93] Empires also have a powerful cultural impact. The rulers gained support for their rule through cultural displays showing imperial grandeur with dominance over enslaved people being a symbol of how the cultural project of empire could be expressed.

---

[90] Paul A. Kramer, 'Power and Connection: Imperial Histories of the United States in the World', *American Historical Review* 116 (2011), 1348–91.

[91] Krishnan Kumar, *Visions of Empire: How Five Imperial Regimes Shaped the World* (Princeton: Princeton University Press, 2017), 3, 475.

[92] Stephen Howe, *Empire: A Very Short Introduction* (Oxford: Oxford University Press, 2001), 14.

[93] Garry Runciman, 'Empire as a Topic in Comparative Sociology', in Peter Fibiger Bang and C. A. Bayly, eds., *Tributary Empires in Global History* (Basingstoke: Palgrave Macmillan, 2011), 99.

Another reason for having empire as a principal analytical category in studying slavery is their historical importance. Walter Scheidel stresses how significant empires were globally, territorially and demographically. At its peak in 1270, the Mongol Empire accounted for 24 million square kilometres, while the Russian Empire in 1895 was similar in size, at 22.8 million square kilometres. The British Empire in 1938 amounted to a remarkable 33.6 million square kilometres. Just over eighty years ago, global imperial territorial concentration peaked at 88 million square kilometres, which was two-thirds of the Earth's land mass, excluding Antarctica. The percentage of the world population taken up by the three largest empires in the world was most massive in late antiquity when the Roman, Han and Kushan empires contained some measure of control over as much as two-thirds of all people on the Earth. A millennium later, in 1900, China, the British Empire and Russia accounted for perhaps 60 per cent of the global population.[94] What this implies is that a very large percentage of enslaved people – probably greater than the percentage of the global population in empires overall as slavery was not common in most hunter-gatherer societies – lived in empires. Scheidel estimates that the Roman Empire was easily the largest slave society in history. He notes that if the Roman Empire contained several million slaves for twenty or more generations, then the total number of enslaved people who lived in the Roman Empire would have been between 100 and 200 million. By comparison, J. David Hacker estimates that 9,979,728 enslaved people lived in North America – America's largest slave society – during the seventeenth through the mid-nineteenth centuries.[95]

Empires, of course, despite their protean nature and their tendency towards multiculturalism and the management of diversity, were not kind places. Violence was central to how empires governed diverse kinds of peoples and slavery was a tool through which violence could be exercised. There is a continual battle between empire as a source of oppression and enslavement and empire as the bedrock of peace and prosperity, the foundation of law and civilisation. The politics of difference within empires took many forms, from difference being celebrated to difference being a justification for genocide. The history of Atlantic slavery shows how easily the politics of difference could become the politics of race. As Francisco Bethencourt argues, while prejudice and stereotyping can exist in any kind of society, in the specific context of

---

[94] Walter Scheidel, 'The Scale of Empire: Territory, Population, Distribution', in C. A. Bang and Walter Scheidel, *Oxford World History of Empire 1*, 92–4, 97, 102.

[95] Walter Scheidel, 'Slavery', in Walter Scheidel, ed., *Cambridge Companion to the Roman Economy* (Cambridge: Cambridge University Press, 2013), 90; J. David Hacker, 'From "20. and odd" to 10 Million: The Growth of the Slave Population in the United States', *Slavery & Abolition* 41 (2020), 845.

Atlantic slavery, elites transformed racial distinctions into ideologies of systematic subordination, exploitation and exclusion. Racism was thus a consequence of certain kinds of imperialism, a mode of thinking that evolved in conjunction with the exercise of power and exploitation.[96] The desire for 'race' to be clear cut and for racial 'purity' to be self-evident, however, ran up with the reality of miscegenation, which was close to inevitable in empires characterised by difference. An entire genre of paintings, for example, in Spanish America – the 'castas' paintings – pointed to how Indians, Europeans and Africans mated together, complicating any easy notion of races separate from each other.[97]

From ancient times, slavery has been associated with imperial expansion and the conquest of subject populations. Indeed, slavery and imperialism were generally compatible and mutually reinforcing for most of their long histories. It is hardly surprising that slavery is an intrinsic part of most empires as empires were institutions that imposed their rule upon a multicultural and multi-ethnic set of populations living in a diverse area. What was central to most empires was that the metropolis thought itself culturally superior to the colonial subject populations and forced the colonies to be under metropolitan control. In traditional empires, 'it was not unusual for ethnically alien conquerors to recognise openly, and rely upon, the cultural and administrative superiority of subjugated peoples' to provide services that the metropolis could not. The reverse, however, is true in modern empires which have a 'civilising' aspect to them, which often meant seeing enslavement 'outside' the metropolitan centre as a necessary evil for as yet 'uncivilised' people.[98]

Slavery flourished in empires. It was clearly deeply embedded in the lives of ancient Mediterranean empires, was strongly connected to expansion in the Roman and Ottoman empires and was especially important in Atlantic empires and the plantation societies established in the early modern Americas. Slavery was also important in the Indian Ocean World and its global economy, which was a sophisticated and durable system of long-distance exchange that linked China to Southeast and South Asia, the Middle East and to Africa, even if, as Andrea Major argues, there has been a long-term inclination to see slavery and empire, wrongly, as not closely connected.[99] For the Pacific Ocean world, much

---

[96] Francisco Bethencourt, *Racisms: From the Crusades to the Twentieth Century* (Princeton: Princeton University Press, 2013).

[97] Rebecca Earle, 'The Pleasures of Taxonomy: Casta Paintings, Classification, and Colonialism', *William and Mary Quarterly* 73 (2016), 427–66.

[98] Thomas T. Allsen, 'Pre-modern Empires', in Jerry Bentley, ed., *The Oxford Handbook of World History* (Oxford: Oxford University Press, 2011), 363.

[99] William Gervase Clarence-Smith, ed., *The Economics of the Indian Ocean Slave Trade in the Nineteenth Century* (London: Frank Cass, 1989); Andrea Major, '"The Slavery of East and West": Abolitionists and "Unfree" Labour in India, 1820–1833', *Slavery & Abolition* 31 (2010), 501–25.

emphasis has been put upon bonded labour in the nineteenth century, with South Asians and Chinese moving to Fiji and Hawaii to work on plantations and Pacific Islanders doing similar coerced migrations to cultivate sugar in Queensland.[100] But there was also slavery in New Zealand. Maori were permitted under the Treaty of Waitangi in 1840 to establish a system of slavery that reinforced traditional hierarchal divisions.[101] Slavery still needs to be fully incorporated into histories of empire, perhaps more so than the other way around. The pervasiveness of slavery within the imperial economies of the New World has tended to make theorists of empire underplay its importance.[102]

Nevertheless, the importance of slavery in empire is increasingly recognised. It is seen in museum curatorship, in efforts by historians such as Olivier Pétré-Grenouilleau, Frédéric Régent and François-Joseph Ruggiu in France and, most notably, Catherine Hall in Britain, to insist that slavery is an integral part of French and British history; in major digital projects such as the Legacies of British Slave-Ownership project run by University College, London; and in the ambitious movement by historians of the American nineteenth-century South to conceptualize that region as an American slave empire.[103] The integration of slavery with empire remains patchy and is marked by more heat than light – history as rhetoric more than history as scholarship – with one strand of scholarship on empires hardly mentioning slavery and another making outsized claims for its importance. But the trend is inescapable, which is that as more attention is paid to both historical topics, the more they merge together. Multi-ethnic empires, encompassing populations of differing peoples, languages and confessions, used slavery as one of the many ways of aligning accommodations with difference to imperial rule. Empires thus shaped the terms and experiences of slavery through their very formation, how they interacted with other (usually imperial) polities and through the laws and customs they employed to control, discipline and protect their subjects. Seeing slavery as imperial and imperialism as incorporating slavery might be a useful way forward, especially if gender is paid greater attention as a structuring element of such accommodations and rules, from the increasingly problematic concepts of social death and slave societies which have hitherto dominated thinking on what constituted the essence of enslavement.

---

[100] Tracey Banivanua Mar, *Violence and Colonial Dialogue: The Australian-Pacific Indentured Labour Trade* (Honolulu: University of Hawai'i Press, 2007).

[101] Hazel Petrie, *Outcasts of the Gods? The Struggle Over Slavery in Māori New Zealand* (Auckland: Auckland University Press, 2015).

[102] Trevor Burnard, 'Slavery and Empire', in Doddington and Del Lago, *Writing the History of Slavery*, 59–80.

[103] Ibid., 72–8.

Imperial Examples

Putting empire more closely at the centre of slavery studies has substantial benefits when understanding the spread of slavery and the relationship of enslaved people to wider social and political institutions, as already outlined for early modern Atlantic slavery. The usefulness of empire as an analytical category can be seen just as well in other cases, four of which – the Mongol Empire, nineteenth-century African history, the Ottoman Empire, and ante-bellum US South slavery – are canvassed here.

Slavery in the Mongol Empire benefits in particular from the move towards deeper empirical investigations and a deeper appreciation of imperial themes, allowing scholars to move away from models derived from Marx, Patterson or Finley which do not really work in explaining the role of slavery in this empire. The rise of the Mongol Empire (1206–1368) had a transformative impact upon slavery throughout Eurasia. The pre-imperial Mongols were not notably reliant on slavery, but their massive military campaigns created vast numbers of war captives who were made into slaves. Mongols saw people as a resource to be used for imperial needs no different from material goods. As Michael Biran argues, this sudden expansion of slavery in Mongol-held areas led to the commodification of people, encompassing a range of dependencies from nearly free people to full slaves.[104]

The status of enslaved people varied enormously with talented enslaved people enjoying considerable social mobility. Slavery among the Mongols was essential in how they kept their empire in order, as the low population of pre-imperial Mongolia at 1 million people was nowhere sufficient to rule the largest contiguous empire in world history. The Mongols needed to fully mobilise the resources they had, both human and material. Coercion was key to that mobilisation. The unprecedented scale of the Mongol conquests resulted in a huge increase in slavery and a redefinition of slavery throughout large areas of Eurasia. Biran concludes that 'the slaves took part in the interreligious and intercultural encounters typical of Mongol Eurasia'.[105] The Mongol conquests led to an upsurge in Eurasian slave supply, especially in domestic slavery and in the expansion of the enslavement of women. The Mongol men had a fetish for Korean women and girls, which was noticeable in their relations with the Yuan imperial court in China and the representative of the Guryeo dynasty in Korea. Qubilai Khan, for example, the ruler of China in the late thirteenth century, encouraged intermarriage between Mongols and Koreans. Most Korean women in the Mongol Empire, however, were not wives but were concubines, servants

---

[104] Biran, 'Forced Migrations and Slavery in the Mongol Empire (1206–1368)', 76.
[105] Ibid., 99.

and slaves. It was one way by which Mongol slavery came into congruence with longstanding Chinese conventions.[106]

Another area where slavery and empire are indubitably linked was in the nineteenth-century Sub-Saharan Africa. Slavery was an ancient institution in Africa, but it spread considerably in West and Central Africa during the transatlantic slave trade and as empires developed following jihad from 1804. African slavery was distinctive in its global context with three separate slave trades out of Africa – to the Mediterranean, to the Indian Ocean and to the Americas – as well as an extensive internal slave trade. The enslavement of Africans started early, ended late and played a key role in global modernity. It only ended officially, in Mauritania, in 1981 and illegal slavery remains rife throughout the continent, including much sexual slavery and extensive enslavement of children for military and agricultural purposes.

The geographical diversity of slavery in Africa and the willingness of people throughout much of the continent to acquire, use and dispose of slaves may justify Axelle Mabou's comment that it is only in Africa where we see repeated and significant acceptance of sending people from one's own region and ethnicity to become enslaved in other places.[107] It says something about the mobility of African economies. Richard Roberts comments, for example, about the Segu Bamburu state of the Middle Niger River of interior West Africa between 1712 and 1861 that 'the Segu state, unlike its coastal counterparts, managed to avoid dependence on one primary market. Slaves captured by Segu warriors were sent to the Atlantic, the desert, and to interior markets. Some were retained locally'.[108] Slavery was ubiquitous and increased over time, but it was not all that important in the total African economy. Domestic economies not based upon slavery were always much more important than Africa's foreign trade with many places in Africa, like most of southern Africa and areas around the Great Lakes, like Burundi, functioned without slavery. Moreover, Africa was becoming less significant to the world economy at the same time that it involved itself more closely in international commercial relationships.[109]

In addition, Africans were not always enthusiastic enslavers. There was an abolitionist movement in the kingdom of Kongo in west-central Africa from the late seventeenth century. José Lingna Nafafé details at length the remarkable case that Lourenço da Silva de Menonça, a high royal official, brought to the

---

[106] Don J. Wyatt, 'Slavery in Medieval China', in Craig Perry, David Eltis, Stanley L. Engerman and David Richardson, *Cambridge World History of Slavery 2*, 288–9.

[107] Axelle Kabou, *Et si L'Afrique refusait le développement?* (Paris: L'Harmattan, 1991).

[108] Richard Roberts, *Warriors, Merchants, and Slaves: The State and the Economy in the Middle Niger Valley, 1700–1914* (Stanford: Stanford University Press, 1987), 18.

[109] Ralph Austen, *Trans-Saharan Africa in World History* (New York: Oxford University Press, 2010).

Vatican in 1684. He accused European slave traders of committing crimes against humanity through the tyrannical sale of human beings. It was a highly organised, international-scale legal court case for liberation and abolition, undertaken a century before abolitionism emerged in Europe in the late eighteenth century.[110] In the nineteenth century, a revisionist new history around the Jihad movement that led to the establishment of the Sokoto Caliphate suggests that within Jihad was a significant abolitionist movement and that Jihad was not just a thinly veiled pretext to wage war so as to acquire new sources of slaves.[111] For example, between 1776 and his death in 1806, Abdul-Qadir Kan led a revolution against slavery in the Senegal River Valley state of Fuutu Tora, encouraging Muslim liberation theologies based on the strong calls to manumission he argued were throughout the Quran. As elsewhere in empires, the expansion of slavery in West Africa coincided with stronger commitments to emancipation.

One of the great ironies of the nineteenth century is that the formal abolition of the European slave trade out of Africa led to the dramatic expansion of slavery within Africa. In the European imagination, stereotypes about the cruel Arab slaver made ending slavery in Muslim Africa especially important in how the 'white man' imagined his 'burden' of civilising darker races through emancipation and colonisation. Most European intellectuals wove Africa, Islam, and slavery together in a justification of colonialism. Many Africans, of course, supported both slavery and a colonisation that allowed them to continue slavery while paying lip service to abolitionism. But some African Muslims – left out of the genealogies of modern abolitionism – also criticised slavery, racism and the obvious conjunction of the two through normative Islamic notions of ethical behaviour.[112]

The nineteenth century was the age of slavery and the age of empire in much of Africa, a revolutionary century in which Africa became increasingly integrated into a global economy and subject to European imperialism.[113] That imperialism began informally during the first half of the nineteenth century and was closely connected, first for the British and then for the French, to efforts to stop the Atlantic slave trade. Ironically, the push to abolish the transatlantic slave trade and to do so through imposing imperial rule throughout Africa

---

[110] José Lingna Nafafé, *Lourenço da Silva Mendonça and the Black Atlantic Abolitionist Movement in the Seventeenth Century* (Cambridge: Cambridge University Press, 2022).

[111] Paul E. Lovejoy, 'Islam, Slavery, and Political Transformations in West Africa: Constraints on the Transatlantic Slave Trade', *Revue d'Histoire Outre-Mer* 336–7 (2002), 247–82.

[112] Rudolph T. Ware, *The Walking Qur'an: Islamic Education, Embodied Knowledge, and History in West Africa* (Chapel Hill: University of North Carolina Press, 2014).

[113] Joseph E. Inikori, 'The Development of Capitalism in the Atlantic World: England, the Americas and West Africa, 1450–1900', *Labor History* 58 (2017), 138–53.

coincided with a huge expansion of slavery, not just in areas under European influence but within the continent of Africa. The start of jihad in Central Sudan in 1804 leading to an imperial configuration called the Soko Caliphate and the consolidation of the kingdom of Dahomey in the late eighteenth and early nineteenth centuries greatly increased the extent of slavery in Sub-Saharan North and West Africa. That expansion of slavery continued throughout the century and was enhanced by the late nineteenth century scramble for Africa, whereby slavery was ostensibly outlawed but was in fact able to flourish within territories acquired by abolitionist European empires.[114]

The result was an ideological commitment to abolitionism that was marked by gradualism and an accommodation to slavery that allowed what Frederick, Lord Lugard, a British imperial official in Uganda and Nigeria, called the 'slow death' of slavery.[115] At the same time as it was supposedly slowly dying, slavery intensified in the nineteenth century in many Sub-Saharan places. Slavery became an increasingly essential part of African society and economy in places like the Soko Caliphate, where there were more enslaved people in 1861 than in the Confederate South, in Bugunda in the Great Lakes region and in the Gaza kingdom of southern Mozambique.[116]

Abolitionism and the expansion of slavery were closely connected for two reasons. First, colonialism incorporated Africa more closely into global economic networks. The growth of commodity production, for African markets, like the Hausa textile industry, and for foreign commerce, created labour demands that slavery supplied even when there was a lot of pressure from abolitionists that only African products not made by slaves should be bought. In addition, the end of the Atlantic slave trade (though it still flourished illegally until the 1860s, with 2.8 million West Africans crossing the Atlantic into enslavement compared with 1.2 million slaves entering the Sahara trade and 934,000 becoming enslaved in the Red Sea and Indian Ocean trade) forced Africans to develop other economic activities, such as plantation agriculture. As Gareth Austin comments, the growth of commodity production created labour demands that encouraged slavery, whatever European abolitionist objections were aired. Slave prices rose after having fallen appreciably after 1807 when the

---

[114] Frederick Cooper, 'The Problem of Slavery in African Studies', *Journal of African History* 20 (1979), 103–25.

[115] Paul E. Lovejoy and Jan Hogendorn, *Slow Death for Slavery: The Course of Abolitionism in Northern Nigeria, 1897–1936* (Cambridge: Cambridge University Press, 1993).

[116] Henri Médard and Shane Doyle, eds., *Slavery in the Great Lakes Region of East Africa* (Oxford: Oxford University Press, 2007); Paul E. Lovejoy, 'Jihad and the Era of the Second Slavery, *Journal of Global Slavery* 1 (2016), 28–43; Patrick Herries, 'Slavery, Social Incorporation, and Surplus Extraction: The Nature of Free and Unfree Labour in South-east Africa,' *Journal of African History* 2 (1981), 309–30.

British slave trade was stopped. As Africa's plantation sector grew and became more profitable and more integrated into global markets, the number and value of slave property increased.[117]

In the last two decades of the nineteenth century – the decades of imperial transition – between a quarter and a third of the population of West Africa were enslaved. Paul Lovejoy has explained this rapid rise of slave numbers in nineteenth century West Africa as a social and economic transformation. He argues that slavery, which was less important in previous centuries, especially outside West Africa, grew in the nineteenth century as a result of developing intercontinental trade.[118] Colonisation in Africa did little to end this transformation, except that imperial officials made some desultory efforts to lessen the brutality of slave life and tried to stop slave-derived raiding and warfare, as had characterised the rise of predatory slave regimes like Dahomey under the tyrannical rule of King Ghezo (1818–59). Ghezo successfully fended off British efforts to curb the transatlantic slave trade and used slavery to increase solidarity among those of his people who were free by redistributing wealth and developing slave-based plantations.[119] Emancipation, consequently, when it came in the early twentieth century due to imperial pressures, was a major blow for West African slaveholders forced to pay relatively high wages for former slaves who achieved such wages through having considerable bargaining power, backed by sympathetic imperial governments.[120]

Slavery in the Ottoman Expire

The Ottoman Empire offers a different, though not exactly alternative, model to transatlantic slavery. It is a subject that is attracting more attention than in the past, but the literature on Ottoman slavery is still small and the sources to understand it are underutilised. Indeed, it is a field that is dominated by the work of one scholar, Ehud Toledano, who has produced a series of articles and books about how Ottoman slavery fits into other models of slavery (he finds Patterson unhelpful, but he believes Finlay's idea of societies with slavery to be

---

[117] Bronwen Everill, *Not Made by Slaves: Ethical Capitalism in the Age of Abolition* (Cambridge, MA: Harvard University Press, 2020); Gareth Austin, 'Slavery in Africa, 1804–1936', in Eltis, Engerman, Drescher and Richardson, *Cambridge World History of Slavery 4*, 178–9.

[118] Paul E. Lovejoy, *Transformations in Slavery: A History of Slavery in Africa*, 3rd ed. (Cambridge: Cambridge University Press, 2012).

[119] Patrick Manning, *Slavery, Colonialism and Economic Growth in Dahomey, 1640–1960* (Cambridge: Cambridge University Press, 1982); Robin Law, *The Slave Coast of West Africa, 1550–1750: The Impact of the Atlantic Slave Trade on an African Society* (Oxford: Oxford University Press, 1991).

[120] Benedetta Rossi, *From Slavery to Aid: Power, Labour and Ecology in the Nigerien Sahel, 1800–2000* (Cambridge: Cambridge University Press, 2015).

analytically useful in discussing a society when around 8 per cent of the population were enslaved, including some who were of very high status).[121]

Enslavement in the Ottoman Empire is important because the Ottoman Empire was the most important Islamic power between the mid-fifteenth to the late nineteenth century. Its territory stretched at its peak from the western Mediterranean to the Persian Gulf and from southern Poland to southern Sudan. The numbers involved in Ottoman enslavement were considerable. From the sixteenth to the eighteenth century, the two major reservoirs of imported slave labour were the Ukrainian steppe (from where about 2 million people were drawn) or from the Mediterranean (from where 1.5 million people came to Ottoman lands). In the eighteenth and nineteenth centuries, the major sources of slavery were Caucasians, mainly from Circassia and Georgia, as well as Africans, from the Nile Valley.[122]

Its differences from transatlantic slavery have led to a fruitless debate about whether enslavement in the Ottoman Empire was milder than in the Atlantic world. In an Indian Ocean model, resistance to slavery was less intense, with enslavement tending towards being a temporary state while enslaved people were integrated into mass society.[123] Notions of mildness underplay, however, the extent of mistreatment of the majority of non-elite female domestic slaves, reflecting too much Muslim apologists both for slavery and also for the absence of any serious abolitionist movement in the Islamic world. It underplays, also, the particularly gendered nature of slavery in societies committed to the maintenance of patriarchy.[124]

In some ways, Ottoman enslavement shared similar attributes to slavery elsewhere; African slaves, in particular, were badly treated, physically and psychologically, and enslaved people showed their opposition to their enslavement through day-to-day resistance. One difference from transatlantic slavery was that Ottoman slavery was an open system of slavery (and we are hindered in appreciating Ottoman slavery through language, as the English words 'slave' and 'slavery' do not cover the range of what Toledano considers as system of Ottoman slavery that was a 'continuum' of forms of servitude and freedom).[125]

---

[121] Ehud R. Toledano, *As if Silent and Absent: Bonds of Enslavement in the Islamic Middle East* (New Haven: Yale University Press, 2007).

[122] Ehud R. Toledano, *Slavery and Abolition in the Ottoman Middle East* (Seattle: University of Washington Press, 1997).

[123] Gwyn Campbell, ed., *Abolition and Its Aftermath in Indian Ocean Africa and Asia* (London: Routledge, 2005).

[124] Madeline C. Zilfi, *Women and Slavery in the Late Ottoman Empire: The Design of Difference* (New York: Cambridge University Press, 2010).

[125] Ehud Toledano, 'The Concept of Slavery in Ottoman and Other Muslim Societies: Dichotomy or Continuum?' in Miura Toru and John Edward Philips, eds., *Slave Elites in the Middle East and Africa: A Comparative Study* (London, 2000), 159–75.

Slaves became gradually integrated into the Ottoman society, especially as manumission was mandated to occur, and often did so, after five to seven years of enslavement.

Some enslaved people in the Ottoman Empire, unlike in the Atlantic world, were of high status. The sultans in charge of the empire invented a system of *devshirme*, or the enslavement of promising peasant children to serve in the sultan's court. *Devshirme* allowed a few poor people a route to power, wealth and a career within the Ottoman state. Many grand viziers, for example, were *devshirme*. It was a way for sultans to bypass involvement with aristocratic dynasties by creating a political class with undivided loyalties to the sultanate.[126]

The integrative nature of Ottoman enslavement, with high rates of manumission and with it being essentially a kind of patronage relationship formed and often maintained by coercion but requiring a measure of exchange that posited a complex web of reciprocity, was compounded by much enslavement being largely domestic and female centred. Manumission was principally a means of including women into Ottoman society securing the lineages that women created through concubinage. Ottoman enslavers, who tended to prefer White women, thus Circassians, for concubinage rather than Africans, who were relegated to domestic service, wanted to create large households with a number of dependents. They also needed, as a result of extensive manumission, to fill an almost continuous labour shortage through new stocks of enslaved people. The slave trade to the Ottoman Empire was thus large and extensive. There was no capacity to replenish the supply of slavery internally. Toledano argues that enslavement was a crucial unifying factor in the Ottoman Empire. It brought together male and female, rich and poor, powerful and powerless, rural and urban, Muslim and non-Muslim and people from as far dispersed places as Central Africa and the Eastern Caucasus, through having a 'shared legal status of bondage, with the variety of social impediments it extended in each predicament'.[127] The study of slavery in the Ottoman Empire is a good example of how the studies of slavery and empire are mutually reinforcing.

Imperialism is also a significant factor informing a most unlikely field in slavery studies, the history of slavery in the antebellum US South. For forty years, scholars studying this region have been preoccupied with delineating internal differences between different parts of the South, in portraying the

---

[126] Nur Sobers-Khan, *Slaves without Shackles: Forced Labour and Manumission in the Galata Court Registers, 1560–1572* (Berlin, Klaus Schwarz Verlag 2014).

[127] Ehud Toledano, 'Enslavement in the Ottoman Empire in the Early Modern Empire in the Early Modern Period', in David Eltis and Stanley L. Engerman, eds., *The Cambridge World History of Slavery: Vol. 3: AD1420–AD1804* (Cambridge: Klaus Scwharz Verlag, 2011), 25.

institution of slavery as 'peculiar' and intensely local and in seeing slave owners and sometimes enslaved people as concerned overwhelmingly with the domestic rather than the wider world. This historiographical orientation has reflected the exceptionalist tendency in US history, a tendency that has not altogether disappeared. Yet what Rosemary Zagarri has termed the 'global turn' in the history of the early republic and which has also extended to the study of the antebellum and Civil War periods has led to a renewed emphasis on colonialism and imperialism in the USA.[128]

The new attention to imperialism shows that the end of British imperial rule in 1783 did not mean the end of empire in the USA, even though the new nation was nominally post-colonial rather than colonial.[129] A host of studies have stressed how the American South in the nineteenth century was not an insular republic disconnected from larger global patterns and from imperialism. Walter Johnson, Brian Schoen and Sven Beckert have shown how southern commitment to slave-grown cotton meant that the US South was involved extensively and enthusiastically in multiple global markets, especially linked to imperial Britain.[130] Southern integration into these markets meant that antebellum slave owners saw their security and prosperity in a global framework. This international and imperialist perspective is unsurprising, given the ways in which the South developed out of imperial competition in the American interior and in the lower Mississippi Valley resulting in a vibrant plantation system linked into a broader Atlantic world. The USA did not want to disentangle itself from the deeply entrenched imperial processes that shaped slavery, settlement and sovereignty.

The American South's attitude to imperialism went through several stages, but empire was a constant interest. In the early republic, as the USA joined Brazil and Cuba in 'second slavery', the expansion of slavery occurred in the context of extensive colonisation debates about how to deal with and exclude 'problematic' people in the early Republic – free Blacks and Indigenes in the American interior. Colonisation of free Blacks in places like Liberia, the only US colony in the nineteenth century that became independent, was not identical

---

[128] Rosemarie Zagarri, 'The Significance of the "Global Turn" for the Early American Republic: Globalization in the Age of Nation-Building', *Journal of the Early Republic* 31 (2011), 1–37; David M. Prior, 'Teaching the Civil War Era in a Global Context: A Discussion', *Journal of the Civil War Era* 5 (2015), 97–125.

[129] Jack P. Greene, 'Colonial History and National History: Reflections on a Continuing Problem', *William and Mary Quarterly* 64 (2007), 225–50; John Craig Hammond, 'Slavery, Settlement, and Empire: The Expansion and Growth of Slavery in the North American Continent', *Journal of the Early Republic* 32 (2012), 176–206.

[130] Johnson, *River of Dark Dreams*; Beckert, *Empire of Cotton*; Brian Schoen, *The Fragile Fabric of Union: Cotton, Federal Politics and the Global Origins of the Civil War* (Baltimore: Johns Hopkins University Press, 2009).

to European colonisation as Americans saw their colonisation strategies within the context of establishing republican values outside America.[131]

The second phase of interest in empire came in the aftermath of British abolition of slavery in 1834. Southern slave owners, already attuned to narratives that saw the Haitian Revolution as a grotesque mistake,[132] were horrified by British anti-slavery and emancipation in the Caribbean. They thought that Britain had initiated a contagion of abolitionism and responded by developing an aggressive pro-slavery stance that by the 1840s resulted in a strategy of pro-slavery imperialism. Southern slave owners, as Matthew Karp has shown, established hegemony over US foreign policy.[133] They were emboldened by growing dissatisfaction among French and British industrialists and imperialists about the results of Caribbean emancipation, which was increasingly viewed as a stark failure.[134] Southern slaveholders spearheaded US pro-slavery policies, such as the annexation of Texas in 1848 and made overtures to other American slavery nations like Cuba and Brazil. Politicians in USA interacted especially with officials from Spanish and Portuguese empires as these officials defended the legitimacy of the Atlantic slave trade and plantation slavery in the face of British efforts to abolish the trade and then, from mid-century, to delay and control emancipation in the American places where slavery still existed.[135]

Southerners became increasingly confident in the 1840s and 1850s, developing their own vision of political economy with slavery at its foundation. It was a distinctly imperial vision, seeking to expand southern slavery in Latin America and the Caribbean.[136] This imperial vision meant that southern elites were not beleaguered defenders of a doomed way of life, seeking to desperately defend an archaic institution but advocates for a thriving and modern system of slavery that they believed would contribute to the civilising of the world while advancing global struggle for White supremacy. Indeed, we can see White southerners as embarking upon a bold offensive policy that made them co-progenitors of late nineteenth-century and twentieth-century imperialism that promoted the idea of 'White man's burden' all the way to founding an overseas empire in fact rather than theory. Such optimism on the part of White

---

[131] Brandon Mills, *The World Colonization Made: The Racial Geography of Early American Empire* (Philadelphia: University of Philadelphia Press, 2020).

[132] Matthew Clavin, *Toussaint Louverture and the American Civil War: The Promise and Peril of a Second Haitian Revolution* (Philadelphia: University of Pennsylvania Press, 2009).

[133] Matthew Karp, *This Vast Southern Empire: Slaveholders at the Helm of US Foreign Policy* (Cambridge, MA: Harvard University Press, 2016).

[134] Edward B. Rugemer, *The Problem of Emancipation: The Caribbean Roots of the American Civil War* (Baton Rouge: Louisiana State University Press, 2008).

[135] Christopher Schmidt-Nowara, 'Empires against Emancipation: Spain, Brazil and the Abolition of Slavery', *Review (Fernand Braudel Center)* 31 (2008), 102.

[136] Karp, *Vast Southern Empire*.

southerners might seem misplaced and unrealistic, given our knowledge of later Confederate defeat but was a firm part of the new Confederate state's planning in 1861–2 for the future while engaged in a titanic war with the USA. Adrian Brettle argues that southern thinkers in this period thought that a new Confederate nation would develop its new southern-based empire and would link with other empires, notably the British and Spanish, looking to expand into Cuba and Mexico, thus satisfying the European need for cotton and sugar.[137]

Race and Empire

Taking an imperial approach to slavery also allows insights into one of the most vexed issues around slavery, which is the extent to which enslavement was based on racial discrimination. Race and empire were indelibly linked in the second half of the nineteenth century, meaning that to study either race or empire means having to know a lot about both topics. It was the start of a seventy-five-year period of scientific racism as well as the highpoint of imperial schemes of social engineering that culminated in the eugenics of the Nazis and the Soviet Union in the 1930s and 1940s. It was also a period dominated by empire and imperial thinking, not least about slavery and race. Confederates in the American South in the 1860s dreamt of empires with slavery. Others, more influential than southern planters, argued for empires in which slavery had gone. But empires without slavery were not to be empires of racial equality, at least in European overseas empires and in the USA. Imperial planners did their best, especially in the anglophone world, to clearly demarcate empires by race and geography. Canada, the American North and Southern Australia and New Zealand were to be places of White settler colonialism, with Blacks excluded. Tropical and semi-tropical places in the empire, from Sierra Leone to the West Indies to the American South and to Northern Australia, were to be where post-emancipation Blacks were to be concentrated and kept as a subordinated work force of unskilled labourers, producing goods for the metropole and segregated as much as possible from the White settlement. In short, post-emancipation policies in the anglophone empires justified a racialised geography that divided a set of White settler colonies from Black tropical locations.[138]

Empire does not explain everything to do with slavery – scholars have moved away from monocausal explanations for how slavery started, developed and

---

[137] Adrian Brettle, *Colossal Ambitions: Confederate Planning for a Post-Civil War World* (Charlottesville: University of Virginia Press, 2020).

[138] Ikuko Asaka, 'African American Migration and the Climatic Language of Anglophone Settler Colonialism', in Kristin Hoganson and Jay Sexton, eds., *Crossing Empires: Taking US History into Trans-imperial Terrain* (Durham: Duke University Press, 2020), 207.

ended as the wealth of empirical information makes modelling systematically difficult. But as these case studies show, empire is a useful way on which many aspects of slavery might be explored.

3 Lived Experience

Survivor Tales

In this section, we look closely at an enslaved person's lived experiences. Let us dive in with some stories.

In 2018, Nadia Murad was awarded the Nobel Peace Prize for her efforts to end the use of sexual violence as a weapon of armed conflict. What is notable about Murad is that she had been a slave. She lived in northern Iraq, an adherent of the Yazıdı religion, which is a syncretic religion combining elements of Islam, Christianity and ancient Iranian religions. In 2014, she was captured by Islamic State militants contesting power in northern Iraq. They claimed that they had the right to treat Murad as an enslaved person because they believed that the Yazidi were devil worshippers. Murad was held as a sex slave, was raped and threatened with execution unless she converted to the Islamic religion. She managed to escape in 2015, fleeing to Germany. She chose to tell her story in a bestselling memoir, *The Last Girl*. Since then, she has become an anti-slavery activist and the first United Nations Goodwill Ambassador for the Dignity of Survivors of Human Trafficking.[139]

The Near Eastern region Murad comes from has a very long history of slavery. The first enslaved person we have any records for was a woman from Assyria named Ahat-abiša who lived in 652 BCE. Her father owed a man named Zabadî thirty silver shekels and gave his daughter as a slave in payment of the debt. We know no more than this about Ahat-abiša, her fate being recorded in cuneiform script on a clay tablet, but that is more than we know about almost any individual from the very distant past.[140]

Some enslaved people were very famous, few more so than St Patrick, who brought Christianity in the fifth century to Ireland. Patrick was a Christian living in Roman Britain who was captured and transported as a slave to Ireland. His *Confession* offers a rare first-hand account of a person made enslaved. Noting he was an 'uneducated sinner', he detailed how at the age of 16 he was captured in the village of Bannavem Taburniae, probably in present-day Cumbria, and

---

[139] www.nobelprize.org/prizes/peace/2018/murad/facts/. Genevieve Lebaron, J. R. Pliley and David W. Blight, *Fighting Modern Slavery and Human Trafficking: History and Contemporary Policy* (Cambridge: Cambridge University Press, 2021); and Elizabeth Bernstein, *Brokered Subjects: Sex, Trafficking and the Politics of Freedom* (Chicago: Chicago University Press, 2019).

[140] Davis, *Slavery and Human Progress*, 8.

'was led into captivity in Ireland along with so many thousands of people'. It was a fate, he declared, that he deserved, having 'fallen away from God' and being 'not obedient to our priests, who were warning us for our safety'. He was put to work, for six years, as a shepherd, where he found God again. One day, he received a God-sent message and ran away from his master, walking 200 miles to the Irish coast where he caught a ship to England. His family wanted him to stay in his home village, but Patrick had a vision, imploring him to return to Ireland with a mission to convert pagans into Christians. That Patrick had been a runaway slave who had not expressed remorse for absconding disturbed later commentators. A biography from the late seventh century by Muirchû moccu Machlténi included an apocryphal story about how Patrick had tried to pay his old master for his value as a slave, but his former master allegedly set himself on fire 'so that he not become subject to his own slave'.[141]

A much darker tale of slavery from Russia in the tenth century is one about the ritual torture and execution of a nameless female slave. It comes to us from the writings of the traveller, Ibn Fadlan, who was sent from Baghdad by the Abbasid caliph, Al Muqtador, in 921 to observe the Volga Bulghars in the territory of the Rus. One part of his account is notorious. It is a detailed description of the funeral of a Rus chieftain. The funeral was conducted by a woman referred to as 'the Angel of Death', who was described by Ibn Fadlan as 'a witch, thick bodied and sinister'. An important part of the funeral ceremony was that someone needed to accompany the chieftain to the afterlife. A girl volunteered to be sacrificed, although it is hard to know the extent to which she was a willing volunteer given that she was plied throughout the gruesome ceremony with alcohol and drugs. The girl was raped repeatedly by the chieftain's men, who claimed that they did this out of love for their dead chief.[142] One potential reason why she may have done what she did was that through this ritual the slave girl was promoted, if briefly, from the status of a slave to the status of a bride-in-death of a chieftain. But her end was horrible. She was led into a burial chamber and held down by men while others beat their shields to drown out her screams. Then the 'Angel of Death' murdered her. The slave girl's body and the boat she was on were burnt. It was on the one hand, Ibn Fadlan wrote, glorious theatre; on the other hand, it was appalling sustained torture and misogyny.[143]

---

[141] Judith Evans Grubb, 'Child Enslavement in Late Antiquity and the Middle Ages', in Craig Perry, David Eltis, Stanley L. Engerman and David Richardson, eds., *The Cambridge World History of Slavery: Vol. 2: AD 500–AD 1420* (Cambridge: Cambridge University Press, 2021), 157–9.

[142] For a later example, see Tamar Herzig, 'Slavery and Interethnic Sexual Violence: A Multiple Perpetrator Rape in Seventeenth-Century Livorno', *American Historical Review* 127 (2022), 194–222.

[143] Paul Lunde and Caroline E. M. Stone, *Ibn Fadlan and the Land of Darkness: Arab Travellers in the Far North* (London: Penguin, 2011), 45–54; Cat Jarman, *River Kings: The Vikings from Scandinavia to the Silk Roads* (London: William Collins, 2021), 209–17.

The sources we often have to use to hear enslaved people are very often highly compromised but can be very rewarding about enslaved experience. Thus, Brett Rushforth has recreated from court records of eighteenth-century Montreal the life of a thirty-year-old Indigenous Canadian enslaved woman, named Marie-Josephe, commonly called Manon, who in October 1750 was accused of stealing a valuable silver fork and spoon from her master and, rather unusually for a slave, given that most masters dealt with enslaved theft summarily, was asked to defend herself in a French imperial courtroom. Two days into the trial, Manon was questioned by officers of the court. Much of the lengthy testimony in the case is very bland, revolving around Manon's name and age with the court officers questioning her about her duties as a servant woman in her owner's house. One of the virtues of the 104-page court record is that it gives great detail about Manon's daily activities, from tasks she did for her master to work she did for herself, to how her activities were subject to Montreal's invasive shared surveillance intended to keep enslaved people under control and about a few stolen moments of private conversation and camaraderie. Another feature of the court record is what is noted about Manon's many associates, illustrating how networks of the poor, the ordinary and the unfree interacted with each other. Her community included soldiers, domestic servants, apprentices and a circle of friends that consisted of French-Canadian young adults, who were temporarily bound together with advantages that pertained to free people which were denied to Manon. Manon was absolved of theft but died, eleven years later, as an enslaved woman with no family or property of her own.

Manon's evidence gives us a rare opportunity to see how an enslaved woman, in a position of jeopardy and liable to punishment, marshalled her friends and acquaintances to give testimony in her favour so that she might persuade the court that 'her answers contained the truth'. Her ordeal allows us to briefly enter into the world of an enslaved native Canadian woman and understand through her evidence the relationship between performance and authority. As Rushforth argues, the court record 'allows us to eavesdrop on one moment in Manon's struggle with those in power' and to 'listen with her' as she heard the words she had said repeated back to her by the careful recording of the clerk of the court, done in real time.[144]

Finally, we can examine the case of Lucile, a forty-year-old seamstress, living in Guadeloupe in 1840, in the last days of French slavery. Her testimony, also from court records, offers us a way to evaluate a key theme in the history of

---

[144] Brett Rushforth, '"She Said Her Answers Contained the Truth": Listening to and with Enslaved Witnesses in Eighteenth-Century New France', in Sophie White and Trevor Burnard, eds., *Hearing Enslaved Voices: African and Indian Slave Testimony in British and French America, 1700–1848* (London: Routledge, 2020), 119–42.

slavery – the range of forms of violence, both day-to-day and exceptional. Lucile was in a court system that allowed enslaved people redress against their masters. Thus, we are able to learn about violence from the perspective of an enslaved person rather than, as is usual, of enslavers throwing enslaved people alive into ovens, burning them alive or killing by slow deaths in gibbets or of slave ship captains torturing captives to death.[145] Lucile started her testimony by praising her master's previous behaviour to her. She noted that this behaviour changed abruptly as soon as she asked him to fulfil a promise he had made to her that he would free her. Her master, she contended, became a different and more hostile person, telling her that she was a 'miserable wretch'. He ordered her, Lucile stated, to 'go rot in the dungeon'. Her master locked her up in an iron ring that was 'extremely powerful' and then deprived her of food and water. 'Without the help of my children', Lucile asserted, 'they would have left me in my garbage, and I was covered with vermin'. She was locked up for twenty-two months and, when freed, 'could not bear the light'. Her legs buckled and she vomited.

Lucile was asked questions from the president of the court and she confirmed that she had not been given sufficient food and declared that she was so certain she was going to perish that she asked for a priest, 'to die at least as a Christian'. This request, however, was denied. Her master claimed that Lucile was a poisoner (which was a common theme within French Atlantic slavery)[146] and was responsible for four of his slaves dying from eating 'dead beef'. Lucile argued that the meat was corrupt and that her master had tried to pin his own failures onto her and another female slave called Quetty. Lucile succeeded in her complaint and was presumably freed. What consequences the master faced for his mistreatment of Lucile is unknown.[147]

Recent work on enslaved people as individuals demonstrates that there are many more sources explicating enslaved experience of people living before the nineteenth century than scholars have thought.[148] It does not mean that such sources are not without sizeable methodological problems. Scholars looking at

---

[145] Trevor Burnard, 'Terror, Horror, and the British Atlantic Slave Trade in the Eighteenth Century', and Cécile Vidal, 'Violence, Slavery and Race in Early English and French America', in Robert Antony, Stuart Carroll and Caroline Dodds Pennock, eds., *The Cambridge World History of Violence: Vol. 3: AD1500–AD1800* (Cambridge: Cambridge University Press, 2020), 15–35, 36–54.

[146] John Garrigus, '"Like an Epidemic One Could Only Stop with the Most Violent Remedies": African Poisons versus Livestock Disease in Saint Domingue, 1750–88', *William and Mary Quarterly* 3rd ser. 78 (2021), 617–52.

[147] Dominque Rogers, 'Lucile de Guadeloupe, de l'intimeté à l'empoissonnement, 1840', in Dominque Rogers, ed., *Voix d'esclaves, Antilles, Guyane, et Louisiana françaises, XVIIIe-XIX siècles* (Paris: Karthala, 2015), 145–8.

[148] Charles T. Davis and Henry Louis Gates, eds., *The Slave's Narrative* (New York: Oxford University Press, 1985); Robert B. Stepto, *From Behind the Veil: A Study of Afro-American Narrative*, 2nd ed. (Chicago: Chicago University Press, 1991).

slavery before the nineteenth century and outside the American South seldom have canonical texts such as autobiographies that span the arc of a life in which a highly individuated self is explained and asserted. How, then, can we study enslaved experience when, as Nicola Aljoe notes, 'the slave's voice does not yet control the imaginative forms which her personal history assumes in print'? The sources from places and times where the archival record is poor tend to be hybrid, polyvocal and oral and often originate in complicated legal systems. But just because we cannot recover the historical individual through fragmented sources, we can still discover much of value. As Sophie White and myself have argued, drawing from Aljoe's contention that we should not dismiss fragmented testimony as 'a mere body of data', enslaved people were involved in the production of their testimonies; and we cannot just discard slave testimonies because they 'fail to fit the overly high standard of literary authenticity required by those who want to hear an unadulterated voice emanating from a slave's consciousness'.[149]

Hearing the Voices of the Enslaved

I have laboured the point about how many testimonies we have about enslaved people, taking care to show a variety of enslaved people, the different predicaments enslaved people faced and the varying quality of the sources available to historians to examine their lives. An important new theme in the writing of global slavery is that we need to prioritise the voices of the enslaved when writing about slavery. What are called 'survivor voices' are highlighted in studies of contemporary slavery, as seen in the awarding of a Nobel Peace Prize to an ex-slave.[150] When scholars and activists write about modern slavery, they foreground survivor voices so as to get an immediate and direct insight into how individuals, communities and states ought to respond to forced labour, sexual and criminal exploitation and human trafficking. The search for voices of the enslaved has become increasingly prominent in studies of historical slavery, with historians attempting to overcome what Annette Gordon-Reed calls 'history's cruel irony that the individuals who bore the brunt of the system – the enslaved – lived under a shroud of enforced anonymity. The vast majority could neither read or write, and they therefore left behind no documents which are the lifeblood of the historian's craft'.[151]

---

[149] White and Burnard, 'Introduction', in White and Burnard, eds., *Hearing Enslaved Voices*, 5; Nicola Aljoe, *Creole Testimonies: Slave Narratives from the British West Indies, 1700–1858* (New York: Palgrave Macmillan, 2012).

[150] Carole Murphy and Runa Lazzanno, eds., *Modern Slavery and Human Trafficking: The Victim Journey* (Bristol: Bristol University Press, 2022).

[151] Annette Gordon-Reed, 'Slavery's Shadow', *New Yorker*, 23 October 2013.

First-hand testimony from the enslaved has been transformative in the historiography of slavery. One reason why antebellum American southern slavery was so normative in modelling slavery is the plenitude of first-hand testimonies from multiple nineteenth-century slave narratives and on interviews gathered by the Federal Writers' Project under the supervision of the Works Progress Administration in the USA in the 1930s. These first-hand testimonies were especially important in reshaping the historiography of slavery around a paradigm of slaves' agency and resistance.[152] Nevertheless, it is remarkable how seldom historians of slavery until recently have referenced individual enslaved people in their writings. In my and Gad Heuman's *The Routledge History of Slavery* (2011), for example, only one enslaved person – Cuffee, an enslaved African – is referenced in the index while there are two references to myself, double that given to any enslaved person. The four volumes of the *Cambridge World History of Slavery* (2011–21) include no separate chapter on enslaved voices and few references to any individual enslaved person. And the number of references to individual voices increases the more recent volume's publication date. The first volume, from 2011, on ancient history, contains only four references to individual enslaved people and one of those is to Tiro, Cicero's secretary and amanuensis. Aristotle, on the other hand, a major pro-slavery thinker, is noted sixty-one times. The next volume, also from 2011, covering the early modern period, has just four references, including three enslaved persons engaging in slave rebellion. The volume on modern slavery, published in 2013, increases the number of references to eleven. The only volume in which individual enslaved people are noted frequently is the last volume, on medieval slavery, published in 2021, which has twenty-seven individual enslaved people mentioned. One essay, by Judith Evans Grubb, is structured entirely around stories drawn from the enslaved.[153]

Three other authors in this volume provide detailed case studies drawn directly from testimony by or about an individual enslaved person, including, that of Ysabel, done by Debra Blumenthal.[154] Another comes from Shaun Marmon. He writes about the Mamluk historian, al-Maqrizi (d. 1442), who chronicled his young female slave, Sul, the *mulwallada*, whom he purchased 'as a virgin' at the age of 15; mainly, it seems to be an investment rather than for household and sexual services. Unusually, al-Maqrizi spent time educating her, though he seems to have done so mainly in order to increase her price and hence

---

[152] Norman R. Yetman, 'Ex-Slave Interviews and the Historiography of Slavery', *American Quarterly* 30 (1984), 181–210; Kathleen Hilliard, 'Finding Slave Voices', in Mark M. Smith and Robert Paquette, eds., *The Oxford Handbook of Slavery in the Americas* (Oxford: Oxford University Press, 2010), 685–701.

[153] Grubb, 'Child Enslavement'.   [154] Blumenthal, 'Slavery in Medieval Iberia', 523–5.

his profits when she was to be resold. Sul became transformed from slave to mistress of a household, showing how fluid some slave systems were. Al-Maqrizi relates that Sul was 'renowned for her authority, magnanimity, sound judgement, sensible management and charity'.[155] Similarly, Matthew S. Gordon writes about a young slave woman named Yumn living in early medieval Islamic Egypt. We know about Yumn from a bill of sale in which her 'quality' was assessed through physical examination. Gordon speculates that Yumn was obliged to participate in the sale by having to undergo an intrusive examination. The physical assessment illustrated how her value was based on her ability to do physical (and probably sexual) work. On the one hand, Gordon argues 'her commodification and physical examination underscore the absence of parity' between the owner and the enslaved person. But it also shows that the enslaved 'by virtue of the provision of their labor, were not without the ability to shape the circumstances of their lives, beginning, in this case, at the point of sale'. Slave agency, often seen in relationship to resistance, might also be seen in how enslaved people became part of households and engaged in 'all manner of social integration'. It is also clear evidence of the gendered nature of Middle Eastern slavery, with women more likely to become enslaved than men within a slave system largely based upon women providing sexual and household services. It is probable that Yumn was being examined as much for the absence of 'defects' in her sexual organs and thus her suitability for a busy Middle Eastern sex trade as well as her capacity to undertake physical work in the household.[156]

Prioritising in our analysis the voices of the enslaved is crucial in shaping discourses around slavery and in changing those discourses so that they are 'survivor focused', to use a term common in studies of modern slavery.[157] Finding enslaved voices that are not just fragments of evidence is very difficult for studies of premodern and non-western slavery, but such sources do exist as seen earlier. When these sources are examined with forensic historical techniques, the results can be startling and revealing. Thus, Kim Bok-rae, drawing on litigation unearthed only in 2010 by Sany-hyuk Lim while working in the Presidential Truth Commission on Suspicious Death, has used the trial of the female *yangmin* (or commoner) Damulsari in 1585 to explore the status of Korean *nobi*, or slaves (though the distinction between serf and slaves is porous for early modern Korea). Damulsari, an eighty-year-old woman, took the daring

---

[155] Shaun Marmon, 'Intersections of Gender, Sex, and Slavery: Female Sexual Slavery', in Perry, *Cambridge World History 2*, 204–5.

[156] Matthew S. Gordon, 'Slavery in the Islamic Middle East (c.600–1000 CE)', in Perry, *Cambridge World History 2*, 341–3.

[157] 'VOICES: Narratives by Survivors of Modern Slavery', Voices · Antislavery Usable Past.

step of stating that she was a *nobi* in order to make her children public- or state-owned *nobis*, which would have allowed them to live in a better condition than if they were designated as private *nobis*. Damulsari was found to have lied about her heritage and in 1586 the Naju governor, Kim Sang-il, chastised Damulsari in his judgement as a liar who had 'betrayed her master and surrendered herself as a public *nobi*'. He argued that 'she deserves a flogging', but he exempted her from punishment due to her age. The main result was that the child and six grandchildren of Damulsari were confirmed as private *nobi* and were thus condemned to hereditary enslavement under the direct control of a noble owner. Bok-rae was able to use this lawsuit as a window to explore the status and history of *nobi*. He argues that this history fits uneasily into histories of slavery predicted upon Atlantic models. Bok-rae concludes that 'her case can be taken as indicative in a micro-historical level of a broader historical truth: it is risky to neglect the diversity of global systems of servitude by attempting to lump them together under a single concept of unfreedom'.[158]

Can the Subaltern Speak?

Natalie Zacek notes that our answer to the famous question that the literary theorist Gayatri Chakravarty Spivak posed a generation ago – 'Can the Subaltern Speak?' – is a cautious 'yes, but'.[159] We seldom get to the voice of the enslaved directly, and even then we have to understand the context in which enslaved people were talking and how dangerous unguarded speech might be for an enslaved person to utter. Miles Ogburn warns how consequential words might be for the enslaved in an instructive story from Barbados in 1683. During an enquiry into a suspected slave conspiracy, an 'old Negro man' declared after seeing rebels whipped until their flesh was in a pulp 'that the Negroes ere long would serve the Christians so'. Such words sufficiently chilled his mistress, Madam Sharp, that the man was burned alive for 'uttering' such 'insolent words'. As Ogburn concludes, 'he suffered and died just for what he said'. And, as Ogburn does not note, the old man remained nameless, while his mistress was given an identity.[160]

---

[158] Kim Bok-rae, 'A Microhistorical Analysis of Korean *nobis* through the Prism of the Lawsuit of Damulsari', in Lemski and Cameron, *What Is a Slave Society?* 396–401, 409. See also De Vito, 'History without Scales', 348–72.

[159] Gayatri Chakravarty Spivak, 'Can the Subaltern Speak?' in Cary Nelson and Lawrence Grossberg, eds., *Marxism and the Interpretation of Culture* (Urbana: University of Illinois Press, 1988); Natalie C. Zacek, 'Voices and Silences: The Problem of Slave Testimony in the English West Indian Law Court', *Slavery & Abolition* 24 (2003), 26.

[160] Cited in Miles Ogburn, *The Freedom of Speech: Talk and Slavery in the Anglo-Caribbean World* (Chicago: University of Chicago Press, 2019), 1.

Like most powerless people, enslaved people learned how to shut up. Few enslaved people were literate so that surviving first-hand testimony from enslaved people is rare, precious and unusual. From extensive immersion in records relating to colonial Jamaica, I have only come across three examples of writings by enslaved people, one of which seems to have come from Virginia and then was misfiled among Jamaican records. That one is a letter from 1723 from an enslaved person in 'verJenna', appealing to the Bishop of London from 'a Sort of people that is Calld Mollaters which are Baptised and brouaht up in the way of the Christian faith', asking that he be given 'Releese' from 'out of this Cruell Bondage'.[161] The next letter from an enslaved person was by an ex-slave called Thomas Foster, who had been given his freedom in the mid-1740s by the Jamaican government for revealing a slave conspiracy. He wrote a pathetic letter from London, where he had removed after being threatened by enslaved people in Jamaica angry at him for being a traitor to the cause of enslaved rebels and where his reputation as a turncoat had preceded him, making him derided, despised and attacked in the metropolis. His plea was for more money to satisfy him for his 'faithful services to the country'.[162] We also hear the voices of enslaved people, albeit as recorded by White officials, in 1765, in a foiled slave rebellion in St Mary's Parish and in 1776 when the Jamaican Assembly initiated an investigation into a large-scale by foiled slave insurrection in Hanover Parish. Several enslaved people were interrogated and tortured and were recorded telling interrogators details about their plans to overthrow White rule in the island.[163]

It is not a surprise that we often read close to direct testimony from enslaved people when enslaved people were in trouble, and especially when they were on trial for their lives. Some of the most vivid testimony from the enslaved we have, for example, comes from the excellent trial records of eighteenth-century Louisiana which have been very usefully exploited by Cecile Vidal, Sophie White and Dominique Rogers. These records, White argues, 'brim with details about daily life and about inner lives … showcasing a multiplicity of voices even if these voices are fragmentary, their autobiographies patchy, their

---

[161] Thomas Ingersoll, '"Releese us out of this Cruell Bondegg": An Appeal from Virginia in 1723', *William and Mary Quarterly* 51 (1994), 781.

[162] Trevor Burnard, 'Une Véritable Nuisance pour la Communauté: La Place ambivalent des libres de couleur dans la société libre de la Jamäique au XVIIIᵉ siècle', in Boris Lesueur and Dominque Rogers, eds., *Sortir de l'esclavage: normes juridiques, assimilations et recompositions identitaires du xIvᵉ au xIxᵉ siècle (Méditerranée, Amériques, Afriques)* (Paris: Karthala, 2018), 173–220.

[163] Devin Leigh and Clifton Sorrell III, 'How to Control the History of a Slave Rebellion: A Case Study from the Sources of Blackwell's Revolt in Sr. Mary's Parish, Jamaica, 1765', *Journal of Caribbean History* 55 (2021), 19–56; Richard B. Sheridan, 'The Jamaican Slave Insurrection Scare of 1776 and the American Revolution', *Journal of Negro History* 61 (1976), 290–308.

concerns those of the moment'.[164] For example, Vidal's analysis of the lengthy lawsuit of Louis Jupiter, accused of running away and theft by breaking and entering in 1744 is based on over 150 pages of testimony.[165]

And it was at these moments, when enslaved were about to lose their lives and when the mask that enslaved people had to wear when dealing with White power slipped that we got some idea of the real feelings that the enslaved had towards their oppressor. Thus, in Barbados, in 1675, a man about to be executed declared bitterly: 'The devil was in the Englishman that he makes everything work; he makes the wind work; he makes the horse work, the ass work, the wood work; the water work and the slave work.'[166] Here in pithy form is a protest about how slavery dovetailed with developing ideas of capitalism and changing notions of work – and an intriguing way in which this condemned man recognised the extent to which Whites saw him as less than a person than as an item in an inventory of tools to make money.

We have huge gaps in our knowledge of the past and especially massive gaps in our understanding of the lives and the thoughts and experiences of ordinary people at almost any place and time. Recovering the voices of such people – rescuing them from the condescension of posterity – has been a constant theme in the historiography of the last century, from the founding of the Annales school by Marc Bloch and Lucien Febvre in 1929 to the development of a history influenced by social science after World War II and especially from the mid-1960s through to the mid-1980s.[167] Indeed, when we go through the immense effort that has been made in seeking out information on the enslaved in the Americas, not least in the Caribbean, one is struck by the quantity of material that is available. There is a lot of information available; the difficulties are in how we access it. But historians have developed methods whereby such stories – the stories of subalterns – can be accessed. Microhistory is a well-established sub-discipline and has led to some magnificent achievements, such as Carlo Ginzburg's *The Cheese and the Worms* or Greg Dening's anthropological explorations of the mutiny on the Bounty in the Pacific.[168]

---

[164] Sophie White, '"Said without Being Asked": Slavery, Testimony and Autobiography', in White and Burnard, *Hearing Enslaved Voices*, 20, 23.

[165] Cecile Vidal, 'Fictions in the Archive: Jupiter Alias Gamelle or the Tales of an Enslaved Peddler in the French New Orleans Court', in White and Burnard, *Hearing Enslaved Voices*, 40–57.

[166] Anon, *Great Newes from the Barbadoes* (London: L. Curtis, 1676), 6–7.

[167] Simona Cerutti, 'Who Is Below? E. P. Thompson, historien des societies modernes: une relecture', *Annales: Histoire, Sciences Sociales* 70 (2016), 943–53.

[168] Carlo Ginzburg, *The Cheese and the Worms: The Cosmos of a Sixteenth-Century Miller*, trans. John and Anne C. Tedeschi (Baltimore: Johns Hopkins University Press, 1982); Greg Dening, *Mr Bligh's Bad Language: Passion, Power and Theatre on the Bounty* (Cambridge: Cambridge University Press, 1992).

But that is not where the methodological and theoretical attention has gone recently. What we have seen in the last decade has been a highly productive series of interventions, with the work of New York-based scholars Saidiya Hartman and Marisa Fuentes prominent, on the problematics of the archive of slavery, with an emphasis on silence and on violence. Of course, this historiography also has a historiography, with inspiration drawn from Black intellectuals dating back to W. E. B. Du Bois and more recently to the Haitian social scientist, Michel-Rolph Trouillot. Trouillot's musings on the silencing of the past especially in relation to the invisibility of the Haitian revolution have an incantatory power for historians interested in connecting the past of slavery to the present and in reflecting on the difficult subject matter of slavery as found in records that smooth over the injustices of slavery into bland, bureaucratic prose. Trouillot insisted that the study of history arose out of an interest in the present, stating that 'historical authenticity resides not in the fidelity to an alleged past but in an honesty vis-vis-the present as it re-presents the past'.[169] He noted that 'history is the fruit of power, but power itself is never so transparent that its analysis becomes superfluous. The ultimate mark of power may be its invisibility; the ultimate challenge the exposition of its roots'.[170]

This concern with the archive as a source of oppression is also reflected in other historiographies that seem to have been unread by American scholars of Atlantic slavery with their relentless American and abolitionist focus. The most obvious parallels are with the Subaltern Studies community of scholars of South Asia, who themselves drew from the work of British Marxist historians such as George Rudé, E. P. Thompson and Eric Hobsbawm in the 1960s 'history from below'. The subaltern school, led by Ranajit Guha, was, as Rosalyn O'Hanlon notes, 'an effort to recover the experience, the distinctive cultures, traditions, identities and active historical practices of subaltern groups [usually considered to be peasants] in a wide variety of settings – traditions, cultures, and practice which have been lost or hidden by the action of elite historiography'.[171] Guha was interested in the consciousness of peasant insurgencies and felt that the sources he was forced to use from colonial archives got in the way of his ambition to restore voice to Indian peasants. He argued that since counterinsurgency and insurgency were the antithesis of each other, the deficient and elite-centred colonial records constitute a mirror that was the inverse of peasant consciousness and thus could be useful, if read against the grain. In effect, if the

---

[169] Michel-Rolph Trouillot, *Silencing the Past: Power and the Production of History* (Boston: Beacon Press, 1993), 148.

[170] Ibid., 14–15.

[171] Rosalyn O'Hanlon, 'Recovering the Subject: Subaltern Studies and Histories of Resistance in Colonial South Asia', *Modern Asian Studies* 22 (1988), 195.

historians reversed what Carlo Ginzburg in another context called the 'archives of repression', then colonial accounts could reveal the authentic peasant or subaltern voice. Of course, as Kim L. Wagner comments, such reinterpreting of the words used by the creators of archival records to describe peasant unrest has its own problems, as it encourages over-reading, in which historians are tempted to find resistance and noble rebels everywhere even when the evidence is too thin to make such assumptions. Such a tendency, Wagner thinks, is probably most strong when 'the historical archive is sparse and so evidently the product of an encounter overdetermined by the imbalance of power'.[172]

The Archive of Slavery

There are some powerful phrases from Hartman that are quoted often to describe what researchers feel on encountering the archive of slavery. Hartman describes this archive memorably. She calls it a 'death sentence, a tomb, a display of the violated body, an inventory of property, a medical treatise on gonorrhoea, a few lines about a whore's life, an asterisk in the grand narrative of history'. Hartman's statement comes at the start of an essay on 'the ubiquitous presence of Venus in the archive of Atlantic slavery' in which she 'wrestles' with the 'impossibility of knowing anything about her except through an archive defined by violence, a violence which dictates Venus' silence'.[173] Hartman meditates on this archive as a 'tomb' by raising a series of questions. 'How', she asks, 'does one revisit the scene of subjection without replicating the grammar of violence. Do the possibilities outweigh the dangers of looking (again) at the violence of the slave trade?' Moreover, she continues, 'how does one recuperate lives entangled with and impossible to differentiate from the terrible utterances that condemned them as property and the banal chronicles that stripped them of human features? And, if so, what are the lineaments of this new narrative?' She reposes the question: 'Put differently, how does one rewrite the chronicle of a death foretold and anticipated, as a collective biography of dead subjects, as a counter-history of the human, as the practice of freedom?' Her answer is twofold: a 'counter-history' which offers a way to 'exceed or negotiate the constitutive limits of the archive' and 'critical fabulation', where she plays with and rearranges stories, 'by re-presenting the sequence of events

---

[172] Kim L. Wagner, 'Resistance, Rebellion, and the Subaltern', in Bang, Bayly and Scheidel, eds., *Oxford World History of Empire 1*, 421; Ranajit Guha, 'The Prose of Counterinsurgency', *Subaltern Studies* 2 (1983), 1–42; Carlo Ginzburg, *Myths, Emblems, and Clues* (Baltimore: Johns Hopkins University Press, 1990), 143.

[173] Saidiya Hartman, 'Venus in Two Acts', *Small Axe* 12 (2008), 1–2; Nicola Aljoe, 'Reading the "Memoirs of the Life of Florence Hall" through the *Long Song* of the Caribbean Colonial Archive', *American Literary History* 32 (2020), 629.

in divergent stories and from contested points of view', so that she can thus exploit the 'transparency of sources', seeing them as fictions of history and thereby enabling her to 'topple the hierarchy of discourse and to engulf author-ised speech in the clash of voices'.[174] She has expanded on this methodological technique in *Wayward Lives*, which emphasises afresh the narrative strategies writers need to employ to get at the experiences of those who have no voices. Hartman advocates for an interpretative strategy which Annette Gordon-Reed, in a sympathetic but critical review, argues gets so close to fiction as to make one speculate why Hartman does not take the final step into imaginative speculation.[175] The principal criticism to make of Hartman is that in her eagerness to overcome the deficiencies in sources, she violates what most historians consider their principal obligation to the past – to be faithful to what we know from sources and not make things up.[176]

Hartman, however, insists that she has a responsibility to the dead that involves imagination in a different way to fiction. As she states, 'The intent of this practice is not to *give voice* to the slave, but rather to imagine what cannot be verified, a realm of experience which is situated between two zones of death – social and corporeal death – and to reckon with the precarious lives which are visible only in the moment of their disappearance.' She is interested in the writing of 'a history of an unrecoverable past; it is a narrative of what might have been or could have been; it is a history written with and against the archive'. She will only go so far in invention, not wanting to 'exceed the limits of the sayable dictated by the archive'. While she insists on experimenting with the narrative, her work on slavery 'depends upon the legal records, surgeons' journals, ledgers, ship manifests, and captains' logs, and in this regard falters before the archive's silence and reproduces it omissions. The irreparable vio-lence of the Atlantic slave trade resides precisely in all the stories that we cannot know and that will never be recovered'.[177]

Hartman's work has an increasingly wide reach, but historians are just as influenced by Marisa Fuentes' observations on how she tried but could not succeed in recovering the lives of enslaved women in early nineteenth-century Barbados. Fuentes outlines vividly the ways in which she found the archive of slavery she was studying ethically concerning, personally troubling and meth-odologically challenging. She admits that she 'went to Barbados searching for

---

[174] Hartman, 'Venus in Two Acts', 4, 10–13.

[175] Saidiya Hartman, *Wayward Lives, Beautiful Experiments: Intimate Histories of Riotous Black Girls, Troublesome Women, and Queer Radicals* (New York: W.W. Norton, 2020); Annette Gordon-Reed, 'Rebellious History', *New York Review of Books*, 22 October 2022.

[176] Trevor Burnard, '"The Righteous Will Shine Like the Sun": Writing an Evocative History of Antebellum American Slavery', *Slavery & Abolition* 36 (2015), 180–5.

[177] Hartman, 'Venus in Two Acts', 12.

something I would never find' and describes how she emerged, a little shell-shocked from the records she was examining, 'empty-handed ... the silence deafening'. It was more than just silence, however, which alarmed her. It was how what material she was able to discover in a highly compromised archive tended to depict women only as victims – 'battered, beaten, executed, and overtly sexualised'. If she was 'searching for the invisible woman', to play on a title of a classic social history book on West Indian slavery by Michael Craton from the 1970s, she found instead a harrowing loss. This archival experience 'provoked' her 'focus on addressing this process of erasure and the violence of their physical, historical and archival condition'. Her challenge was 'to write a history about what an archive does not offer' and her problem was with the materials she found and with a logic of historical writing that 'purported that a history of silence could not be written when there was not enough material to fill an article, let alone a book'.[178]

Her methodological concerns were compounded by what she describes as 'pain' and 'risk', especially 'risk' for someone who was the descendant of enslaved people. She noted that 'confronting sources that show only terror and violence are a danger to the researcher who sees her own ancestors in these accounts' and which entailed for her an immersion in sources that forced her 'to hold and inhabit deep wells of pain and horror'. It was these 'deep wells' that connected her to the present, to how 'people of African descent became disposable, when black lives were objectified and thus vulnerable to the caprice, lusts, and economic desires of colonial authorities' helping her understand how 'the archive and history have erased black bodies and how the legacies of slavery ... [are] manifest in the violence we continue to confront'. Her historio-graphic move is highly productive, but it raises questions about whether the archive of slavery is so compromised by how it was constructed and the silences within it that it means that, as Fuentes states at the end of a book in which she confronts the silences in the archives in a successful fashion, writing proper histories of the enslaved is impossible.[179]

Scholars who draw on Hartman and Fuentes for inspiration express repeat-edly their dissatisfaction with the limitations of the archives and how it is intellectually and physically unsettling. Kelly Wisecup, for example, argues that the archive of slavery 'functions not just as a repository for records and memorials of the past but are [sic] spaces of knowledge production that aim to define what can be known about slavery as well as what kinds of terror and violence are permissible on certain black bodies'. 'As a result', she concludes,

---

[178] Marisa J. Fuentes, *Dispossessed Lives: Enslaved Women, Violence, and the Archive* (Philadelphia: University of Pennsylvania, 2016), 144–7.
[179] Ibid., 146–7.

'working in the archive is always compromised by its propensity to reproduce itself and its ways of seeing'. She sees the archive of slavery as so compromised as needing to be discarded: 'merely expanding the archive or recovering additional texts does not escape the archive and its epistemes'. Thus, we 'need to destabilise the project of the colonial archive itself' by creating projects which 'undercut or compromise their original purposes'.[180] This statement tends towards a nihilism about an archive seen in Foucauldian terms as immensely powerful when it can always be read in ways that go against the archival grain.[181] And it possibly gives too much power to the scholar to determine patterns of reading the historical record.

What some scholars find distressing about the archive of slavery is threefold: its founding origins, as Hartman puts it, in 'a violence that determines, regulates and organises the kinds of statements that can be made about slavery'; its relationship to accounting and usual reduction to quantification, which Jennifer Morgan sees in resulting to a 'perverse arithmetic' in a slave trade 'pervaded' and degraded by 'the metaphors of bookkeeping'; in empirical terms regarding how women enter the archives 'in little more than fragments' with 'snippets of their lives, loves and losses, emerg[ing] from records imputed with the possibility of yielding profits'.[182] Morgan comments, though without providing examples, that 'in the face of a contentious history whose violence continues to animate the present, demography offers a soothing chimera, suggesting that quantifying the totality of the transatlantic slave trade will refute passionate accusations of *maafa* – African devastation caused by the slave trade, underdevelopment, and persistent European and Euro-American extractive violence'. She cautions us against using numbers 'without awareness of how they came to be'.[183] Stephanie Smallwood stresses how the archive of slavery is a representation of power that in itself is unaccountable to the enslaved, stating that the 'silences we encounter in the slavery archive reflect the necessary failure of the attempt to represent subalterns in that idiom'.[184]

---

[180] Kelly Wisecup, 'Panel Introduction: Slavery in the Caribbean – Archives and Representations', *Studies in Eighteenth-Century Culture* 49 (2020), 66.

[181] Ann Laura Stoler, 'Archival Disease: Thinking through Colonial Ontologies', *Communication and Critical/Cultural Studies* 7 (2010), 215–19.

[182] Jennifer Morgan, 'Accounting for "The Most Excruciating Torment": Gender, Slavery, and Trans-Atlantic Passages', *History of the Present* 6 (2016), 188; Sasha Turner, 'The Nameless and the Forgotten: Maternal Grief, Sacred Protection, and the Archive of Slavery', *Slavery & Abolition* 38 (2017), 232.

[183] Jennifer L. Morgan, *Reckoning with Slavery: Gender, Kinship, and Capitalism in the Early Black Atlantic* (Durham: Duke University Press, 2022), 42, 43, 45–8.

[184] Stephanie Smallwood, 'The Politics of the Archive and History's Accountability to the Enslaved', *History of the Enslaved* 6 (2016), 126.

One important tradition that is an influential background to current writings is eighteenth-century Anglo-American abolitionism. This movement is the tradition in which these meditations are written, meditations which follow the tropes and narrative strategies established in the final third of the eighteenth century.[185] That does not mean that there has been a sudden appreciation of abolitionists. Hartman thinks that when Wilberforce denounced John Kimber, the captain of the slave ship *Recovery*, in the House of Commons on 2 April 1792 for flogging to death an unnamed fifteen-year-old from the Niger Delta, he was acting hypocritically, highlighting the violence of the murder for sensationalist, indeed pornographic reasons: 'he wanted the members of Parliament to squirm in their seats, to flinch before her battered body, to recoil with every lash that cut the girl's flesh'. But it is hard to see much difference in what Hartman accuses Wilberforce of doing and how writers influenced by her do when they stress the helplessness of the enslaved person as victim, outline in detail various torments and tortures enslaved women had to endure and concentrate heavily upon sexual violence as a particularly conspicuous and cruel part of the enslaved experience. It is instructive to note that many of the empirical examples of the horror of slavery in recent works were drawn from the lexicon of abolitionist outrage, such as the young woman murdered by Captain Kimber, the horrifying death of a nameless woman on the *Hudibras* and the scandal of the murder of captive Africans to collect on insurance in the *Zong* case of 1783.[186]

Social historians are accustomed to sources being opaque, intransigent and not easy to access. That may be less the case for literary scholars and cultural historians who are used to working their magic on texts that reveal more than the standard materials of social history. Encountering the sorts of material that social historians are used to working with – fragmentary evidence rather than complete narratives – many scholars oriented towards representation recoil at how hard it is to recover evidence. Nicholas Rogers notes how 'Marcus Wood talks of a "white archive" in which African subjectivity is indelibly entangled and emasculated' while commenting, perhaps a bit acidly, that 'others follow Foucault in defining the archive as a citadel of surveillance, perhaps with a Derridean twist ... in which the archive appears as a series of sequestered sites of uncertainty'. He observes that Marisa Fuentes found the evidence found

---

[185] Brycchan Carey, *British Abolitionism and the Rhetoric of Sensibility, Writing, Sentiment and Slavery, 1760–1807* (London: Palgrave Macmillan, 2005).

[186] Hartman, 'Venus in Two Acts'; Sowande' Mustakeem, *Slavery at Sea: Terror, Sex, and Sickness in the Middle Passage* (Urbana: University of Illinois Press, 2016); Brown, 'Social Death and Political Life in the Study of Slavery', 1231–2; Stephanie Smallwood, *Saltwater Slavery: A Middle Passage from Africa to American Diaspora* (Cambridge, MA: Harvard University Press, 2007).

in parliamentary inquiries into the slave trade 'impenetrable, fixated on the horror of slavery at the expense of the slave's suffering and subjectivity'. By contrast, he asserts that the 'agency of slaves is not occluded from the archive'. Nor, he argues, is the archive 'as monolithic or Kafkaesque as it might appear'. There is a lot of information available, including in parliamentary inquiries, which historians can find 'a welter of information' which they are able, based on training in social history methodology, to 'read against the archival grain' so as to 'tease out for marginal groups what Antoinette Burton calls "the fragmented and fugitive traces of historical subjectivity"'.[187]

The methodological perspective that emphasises the ways in which enslaved people were trapped within the tyranny of a restrictive archive thus underestimates enslaved people's capacity for agency. As Nicholas Rogers argues, 'these perspectives are too bleak, too top down and privilege too much victimhood over agency, the administrative gaze over the tactics of the oppressed'. He suggests that such accounts also take too much for granted Orlando Patterson's concept of slavery as social death, as seeing enslaved people as natally alienated and cast adrift from psychological safety in a landscape of terror where White power structures kept them enchained.[188] Many scholars find Patterson's concept no longer very useful in looking at global slavery, as we have noted earlier.[189] Hartman is correct to argue that we find counter-narratives to the standard descriptions of enslaved people. We might start from the actions and words of the enslaved, many of whom refused to conform to expectations about how they should behave, about what they should believe and about how they were instructed to keep silent. Enslaved people often spoke and it is the historian's job to try to hear what they said. The several stories of the enslaved presented at the start of this section show how such materials are available for historical investigation.

Modern Slavery and the Survivor Voice

Survivor narratives have become an important source also in shaping scholarship in modern slavery, which also might serve as methodologies suitable to studying historical slavery. They draw on the experience of historic slavery but

---

[187] Nicholas Rogers, *Murder on the Middle Passage: The Trial of Captain Kimber* (Woodbridge: The Boydell Press, 2020), 180–2; Marcus Wood, *Blind Memory: Visual Representation of Slavery in England and America 1780–1865* (Manchester: Manchester University Press, 2000); Fuentes, *Dispossessed Lives*, 126–7, 142; Antoinette Burton, ed., 'Introduction', in Antoinette Burton, ed., *Archive Stories: Facts, Fictions, and the Writing of History* (Durham: Duke University Press, 2006), 14.
[188] Patterson, *Slavery and Social Death*, 13.
[189] James H. Sweet, 'Defying Social Death: The Multiple Configurations of African Slave Family in the Atlantic World', *William and Mary Quarterly* 70 (2013), 251–72.

also illuminate the ways in which we can build on historical narratives to understand present-day survivors.[190] They increase public awareness and thus drive approaches to contemporary abolition.[191] As Andrea Nicholson argues, 'their enthusiastic voices expose the internal landscape of survivors, unearthing the subtle and complex facets of enslavement, discovery and freedom while their accounts offer us access to the past through the perception of the slaves' own reality'.[192]

One of the most revealing published modern slave narratives is by Mende Nazer, a Nuba woman enslaved as a girl in Khartoum, Sudan who was eventually liberated and moved to London. It took her some time to realise she was enslaved, only doing so when she overheard her mistress call her a slave and say she owned her. It made her feel worthless, 'no longer valuable as a human being', and worse than an animal as cats and dogs get stroked and loved and she had no such comfort. She felt that 'I was a non-person. I didn't really exist.' She fell into despair and coped by identifying with the family that mistreated her rather than her real family, whose fate after the raid from which she was made a slave was unknown to her. She felt alone: 'there was no-one that I could turn to talk about the past – to remember the laughter and the love, to reaffirm my true identity'. Her difficulties with her identity continued even after liberation. She found freedom 'so precious and I would not give it up for the world' but 'never anticipated how difficult it would be for me to change my mindset from being a captive to being a free person, or how complicated life could get in the process'.[193]

Andrea Nicholson has analysed 200 contemporary slave narratives, including 31 published autobiographies. She argues that contemporary narratives continue to emulate historic slave narratives in how they are structured and in their intended rhetorical effect. Survivor identity, she suggests, comes more from survivors' post-liberation experiences than from liberation itself and relate closely to how survivors are able to integrate into communities and feel some sense of belonging. She concludes that contemporary narratives have two fundamental roles in shaping campaigns against modern slavery. They are a rich source for understanding modern slavery and provide means to address

---

[190] Laura Murphy, 'The New Slave Narrative and the Illegibility of Modern Slavery', *Slavery & Abolition* 36 (2015), 382–405.

[191] Kevin Bales, *Ending Slavery: How We Free Today's Slaves* (Berkeley: University of California Press, 2007), 26.

[192] Nicholson, *Bearing Witness*, 3.

[193] Kevin Bales and Zoe Trodd, eds., *To Plead Our Own Cause: Personal Stories by Today's Slaves* (New York: Cornell University Press, 2008), 226; Mende Nazer and Damien Lewis, *Slave: The True Story of a Girl's Lost Childhood and Her Fight for Survival* (London: Sphere, 2010), 114–15, 181, 189–90, 197, 201, 226.

it and are themselves an essential process in 'becoming' for survivors, 'enabling an exploration and reformulation of the self as something other than victim and survivor'.[194]

The narratives she studied were permeated throughout by trauma, suggesting that slavery was difficult to escape and overcome. Alicia Heys finds a similar difficulty in overcoming modern slavery for survivors, which she puts down not only to occasionally hostile environments for slavery victims but as inevitable, given the pervasiveness of slavery arising through conflict.[195] As the trafficked Vietnamese woman, Minh Dang, noted in an open letter to an anti-trafficking movement in 2013, her experience was 'like that of a caged animal in a zoo' and her hardest task was re-learning 'that I am human, that I was always human, and that the people out there – you as well as those that hurt me – are also human'. She insists that 'as we incorporate survivors into the antitrafficking movement and encourage them to be at its forefront we need to recognise their humanity'.[196]

Learning from the Voices of the Enslaved

This short Element has made clear that the assiduous work of historians interested in global slavery has greatly expanded the number and range of first-hand testimonies available from enslaved people. Slavery is not, as Hartman argues, the history of an unrecoverable past but is part of what is so common in the historical record – fragments of narratives that seldom are sufficient in themselves but combined with many other sources can be fashioned into a passing facsimile to what happened in the past. We can see just how much material on individuals who are enslaved in the remarkable website, www .enslaved.org. The website contains information on hundreds of thousands of people caught up in transatlantic slavery from the sixteenth to the mid-nineteenth centuries, drawn from numerous databases, especially the new digital journal, the *Journal of Slavery and Data Preservation*, combined together in a single website. Most stories of enslaved people are mere frag-ments – a name, a notation, a dry recording of a death or punishment – but the website also contains fuller life stories 'of enslaved people fighting for their freedom, of the shifting boundaries between enslavement and liberation, and of the dynamics of slave trading, raiding and life'. It is a source biased towards the USA – ninety-four are from America but twenty-seven are from elsewhere. It

---

[194] Nicholson, *Bearing Witness*.

[195] Alicia Heys, *From Conflict to Modern Slavery: The Drivers and Deterrents* (Oxford: Oxford University Press, 2023).

[196] Laura T. Murphy, *Survivors of Slavery: Modern-Day Slave Narratives* (New York: Columbia University Press, 2014), xvii–xx.

demonstrates that records on enslaved people are the opposite of sparse, confirming James Walvin's contention that

> 'one of the many great ironies of slavery: the very system which silenced the voices of the enslaved, which treated them as mere items of trade, also described and documented each and every aspect of their lives, their sufferings and their dying. The end result is that we know more about the enslaved than we do about any of their free labouring contemporaries, for the simple reason that an enslaved person was treated, from start to finish, as a thing, an object, a chattel. And as an object he or she entered the commercial documentation'.

We know a great deal, therefore, about enslaved people because they were people who were owned and who thus were 'registered, described, and accounted for' by their owners. The result is that 'all this is recorded in ways rarely documented for free labouring people of the same eras'.[197]

Cécile Vidal makes clear how abundant evidence from enslaved people can be in a case study of Louis Jupiter, a twenty-five-year-old enslaved person accused, in 1744 in New Orleans, of running away and of multiple thefts. She follows the example of Natalie Zemon Davis in her famous sixteenth-century collection of the narratives of convicted criminals in describing how Jupiter produced multiple narratives of justification which the historian then fuses together to produce a single narrative. She explains how the amount of material produced in a colonial trial and the time and care that magistrates took in interrogating, listening to and recording what enslaved people had to say, often at great length, can be explained in three ways. First, the monarch (and thus his representatives) was responsible for slave order because the code of conduct for slavery – the *Code Noir* – was a royal document. Second, lengthy trials were an occasion for local authorities to collect information not just about enslaved people but about the whole lower orders so that they could prepare themselves for possible collaboration between Blacks and poorer Whites and for any unrest or slave rebellion. Third, the courts took their role as providers of justice seriously and interrogated enslaved people at length, not because they wanted to confirm decisions already made and inflict severe punishment but because they wanted to enforce justice.

What this evidence provides, even though it is not written by the enslaved, Vidal argues, is that 'taken together, all the tales told by enslaved men and women ... represent a slave counter-narrative to their masters' views'. When judges asked them questions, enslaved people, like Jupiter, constructed stories

---

[197] James Walvin, *A World Transformed: Slavery in the Americas and the Origins of Global Power* (London: Robinson, 2022), xvi–xvii.

that expanded answers to include examples of exploitation and mistreatment. It may have made little difference to the result of court action – Jupiter was convicted and suffered considerable physical punishment – and certainly did not reduce the brutality of state repression. But since enslaved peoples' 'claims asserted their dignity it mattered for their own sake that that they stood up for themselves to present their version of the never-ending struggle between masters and slaves'. Vidal concludes that 'as judicial archives offer a repertoire of daily interactions between people of all conditions, they call for a relational social history of slavery rather than for an impossible quest of individual subjectivity'.[198]

The easiest option when considering weaknesses in archival texts in which almost all surviving archival documents were written by enslavers – people who saw the enslaved either as commodities or inferior people – is to throw up one's hands and consider the sources we use as wholly inadequate to the task. It has led some scholars, notably and surprisingly, scholars expert in the most well-documented period of slavery – nineteenth-century African American history – to claim that there is so little evidence for Black lives that Blacks will always be invisible and that, as Leslie M. Harris and Daina Ramey Berry note, 'even scholars with rich documentary sources feel they have to start their studies by apologising for the alleged thinness of their source base' which shows 'scepticism of the actual work and of future research possibilities'.[199] Harris and Berry find this need to apologise troubling, in part because of a massive increase in primary sources on Blacks and on slavery in the nineteenth-century American South, many of which have been digitised and thus easily able to be accessed. They are 'frustrated by the almost rote claims of a limited archive' when there is 'an ever-expanding body of materials that is actively being recovered, preserved and made increasingly accessible'. They are 'concerned that the talk of scant material will curb discovery and stunt research in a flourishing field'. They fear that some scholars too explicitly take Saidiya Hartman's argument that because so many tales of enslaved women have been deliberately hidden or deleted from sources or archives, we need to practice feats of imagination which Hartman calls 'critical fabulation' and therefore 'dismiss the possibility of archival research'.[200] I share those fears.

Moreover, as James Sidbury comments, some historians are reluctant to push beyond the boundaries of what sources explicitly state so as to invent a range of possible alternatives to the records created by slave owners without conceding

---

[198] Vidal, 'Fictions in the Archive', 52–5.
[199] Leslie M. Harris and Daina Ramey Berry, 'Researching Nineteenth-Century African American History', *Journal of the Civil War Era* 12 (2022), 429–77.
[200] Ibid., 431, 437.

that they have surrendered to planters' dehumanisation of the enslaved. Scholars who prefer to find new sources about the enslaved and to do painstaking demographic and social-structural analysis of slavery rather than to engage in historical speculation and occasionally invention 'do not do so out of a lack of interest in what lies beyond the documents but do so out of distrust in their ... ability to move too far beyond the written record without falling prey to the temptation to project what we want to find onto the black screen left by the slaves'.[201]

But if an opposite opinion is held – that relying only upon sources that have deficiencies in their creation – 'effectively perpetuates the silencing of enslaved voices' – there are many options outside 'making things up' that can be adopted.[202] Historians have long used imagination and 'reading against the grain' to do historical investigation. They have done so even when they have treated the archival record, in Walter Johnson's words, as 'full of lies' or at best containing multiple truths, in order to do their best to recover enslaved voices.[203] It requires deep reading in archival sources and thinking expansively about where the enslaved appears in the historical record. In short, we have the tools of empirical and quantitative history that we can use to underpin a contemporary element of archivally based imaginative speculation. The silences are not 'dead-ends' in the historical process but 'opportunities for deeper contemplation and for the production of a more ethical narrative that is grounded by, though not ultimately beholden to, the documents that survive'.[204]

How is archivally based imaginative reconstructions done in practice? To finish this Element by returning to enslaved lived experiences, we have two examples from early America – a sexual assault from New England in 1638 and the decision in 1771 by a 'privileged' young male African, Jimmy, enslaved by Thomas Thistlewood in Westmoreland, Jamaica, to get his master to force him to move him out of the master's house into doing field labour. Each case demonstrates how a skilled historian can use scraps of evidence to create stories about the enslaved which, though in part invention, 'are held tightly in check by the voices of the past'.[205]

The New England story has the least evidence. Wendy Warren takes a brief paragraph in the travelogue of John Josselyn who stayed overnight at the house

---

[201] James Sidbury, 'From Periphery to Center in Early American Historiography', *Eighteenth-Century Studies* 56 (2022), 24.

[202] Andrea Livesey, 'Quantitative Histories of Slavery', in Doddington and D. Lago, *Writing the History of Slavery*, 353.

[203] Johnson, *Soul by Soul*, 9, 12.

[204] Devin Leigh, 'The Empirical and the Speculative', *Eighteenth-Century Studies* 56 (2022), 15.

[205] Natalie Zemon Davis, *The Return of Martin Guerre* (Cambridge, MA: Harvard University Press, 1983).

of a slave owner, Samuel Maverick. Josselyn told how an unnamed 'Negro woman' was 'loudly wailing in the own Country language'. She, according to Josselyn, had been a high-ranking woman in Africa but had become enslaved and sent via Providence Island in the Caribbean to live under Maverick in New England. Maverick thought that a woman with her pedigree 'would make for a breed of Negroes' and tried to mate her with 'a Negro young man he had in his house'. The unnamed woman would not have sex willingly with the enslaved man; so Maverick ordered the man to have forced sex with the woman – in short, a rape. It was this rape which was 'the cause of her grief', as communicated to Josselyn.[206]

It is a compelling story but one with little documentation, thus raising more questions than it answers. Warren believes, however, that we can reconstruct the raped woman's life, to some extent. She thinks that the enslaved woman arrived in New England in 1638 on the *Desire*, one of the very few ships bringing Africans in the 1630s to Massachusetts. Otherwise, she is forced to extrapolate from general studies of the enslaved in this place and time rather than from specific information. She thinks that the enslaved woman may have spent some time in the Caribbean before coming to New England and notes that her colour and ethnicity set her apart in the colony, speculating that this probably made her lonely and possibly bullied and ostracised.[207]

For some historians, Warren's speculations go too far: there are a lot of 'might', 'must' and 'perhaps' in her analysis. At times, she gets close to Hartman's critical fabulation. But the speculations are reasonable extrapolations from general evidence. Even so, Warren admits that multiple questions remain, especially about what the raped woman felt about being raped and what the consequences were for the parties involved after the rape was discovered. Warren notes that the assaulted woman followed English law for rape victims – an elaborate process of telling what had happened and showing to people in power signs that she had been raped. Such efforts were handicapped by the woman's lack of English and by her status as an enslaved person. Warren justifies her speculative approach by explaining that historians can only do their best with sources and are thus forced to speculate despite specialised knowledge. She concludes that 'we have known for a long time, a story of New England's settlement in which "Mr. *Maverick's* Negro woman" does not appear; here is one in which she does'.[208]

---

[206] Paul J. Lindholdt, *John Josselyn, Colonial Traveler: A Critical Edition of Two Voyages to New England [1674]* (Hanover: University of New Hampshire Press, 1988), 24.

[207] Wendy Warren, '"The Cause of Her Grief": The Rape of a Slave in Early New England', *Journal of American History* 93 (2007), 1031–49.

[208] Ibid., 1047, 1049.

Cecily Jones has more information about the enslaved male whose life she reveals, which accounts for her being less prepared to indulge in speculation than Warren. Nevertheless, she is similarly encouraged to extrapolate about meaning from the sources she can access in a convincing examination of a boy in adolescent crisis. Her article is about a young man called Jimmy, sixteen years old in 1771, whose life we know about from his purchase from an African slave ship in 1765 to the death of his owner, the Jamaican small farmer and prolific diarist, Thomas Thistlewood, in 1786, when Jimmy was thirty-two and the head of a slave family. All the information Jones has about Jimmy, however, comes from Thomas Thistlewood's reflections, including several examples of Thistlewood being exasperated with his slave and punishing him. Her tale is about a relationship between a master and a slave that was always uncomfortable and which, by 1771, had badly soured. Initially, Thistlewood thought highly of the eleven-year-old slave he purchased in 1765, though he still subjected him to several floggings while still a boy and adolescent. In 1770, he started training Jimmy to be a house slave – a position of some privilege in a slave community and a position which usually promised better conditions, more food and the possible chance of manumission.[209]

But Thistlewood's intention to make Jimmy a house slave failed. Jimmy behaved in ways that Thistlewood thought wrong, antagonising his master to such an extent that Thistlewood had him banished to the fields. If we look at Thistlewood's account alone, Jimmy deserved his fate– usually a punishment as working in the fields was markedly harder than working in the house. Jimmy was frequently drunk and abusive and was involved in a relationship with an enslaved woman called Abba, who was also a frequent sexual partner of Thistlewood. From Thistlewood's perspective, Jimmy was a defiant and rebellious young man, defying his authority, and therefore needed to be punished by being removed from Thistlewood's patronage (and presence). Jones, however, does not just accept Thistlewood's view of Jimmy. She battles against Thistlewood's negative opinion of Jimmy, and Thistlewood's disinterest in the personal lives of his enslaved property outside how they were involved with him. Jones suggests a different interpretation to that presented by Thistlewood, using the words 'perhaps' and 'must' but only when she feels she can make reasoned speculation that can be justified by reading Thistlewood closely. Her reading suggests that it is plausible to see Jimmy as having his own agenda, one

---

[209] Cecily Jones, "'If This Be Living I'd Rather Be Dead": Enslaved Youth, Agency, and Resistance on an Eighteenth-Century Jamaican Estate', *History of the Family* 12 (2007), 92–103; Trevor Burnard, *Mastery, Tyranny and Desire: Thomas Thistlewood and His Slaves in the Anglo-Jamaican World* (Chapel Hill: University of North Carolina Press, 2004), 175–208.

that he was perhaps only dimly aware of, and which revolved around a desire as an adolescent for autonomy and independence. Jimmy, Jones argues, preferred to be sent to the fields rather than having to work in the overseer's house under the direction of a man he had come to hate.

Jimmy was happier, it seems, in the fields than in the house, even though he continued to show examples of adolescent angst and insubordination. As Jimmy moved into his twenties and became the head of a family and, crucially, was physically removed from Thistlewood, he became a leader of the slave community. He became, at least as far as we can tell from Thistlewood's diaries, less visibly angry, being seldom opposed to what Thistlewood wanted and, ironically, became, for Thistlewood, increasingly valuable. When Thistlewood died in late 1786, Jimmy was appraised at £130, more than any other enslaved person in his inventory.[210] Jones' analysis, through combining reasonably abundant documentation with justifiable speculation, makes a valuable contribution to the history of adolescence in enslavement and is a model of how reading sensibly against the grain can put flesh and bone onto otherwise dry statistics that are often our major source of evidence about slaves.

Conclusion

Jimmy was African and in the Atlantic rather than the American slave system. He was badly treated, abused and angry, but he was not Orlando Patterson's natally alienated slave. Scholars of slavery are not yet in a position where they are confident in what types of models of slavery can replace the models by Karl Marx, David Brion Davis, Moses Finley and Orlando Patterson – models no longer sufficient as explanatory models for the massively expanded world of global slavery studies. But as we get more information about the life stories of enslaved people, from ancient Mesopotamia to eighteenth-century Jamaica and to modern northern Iraq, our means of writing the history of global history get richer, if more complicated, and much closer to processes and practices of history as worked out for all kinds of humans in past societies and circumstances. How we study global slavery, paying due attention to contingency and difference, and in concentrating on the voices of those unfortunate people enmeshed in enslavement promises to be a vibrant field of developing scholarship. It might be a cacophony of voices without clear models to follow and well adrift of its antecedents in antebellum America and the ancient Mediterranean, but surely as we learn more about the ubiquity of slavery in the past, we will incorporate it ever more centrally into our historical understandings – slavery as itself normative rather than anything that is peculiar.

---

[210] Douglas Hall, *In Miserable Slavery: Thomas Thistlewood in Jamaica 1750–86* (London: Macmillan, 1989).

Select Bibliography

Robin Blackburn, *The Making of New World Slavery: From the Baroque to the Modern, 1492–1800* (London: Verso, 1997).

John Bodel and Walter Scheidel, eds., *On Human Bondage: After Slavery and Social Death* (Oxford: Blackwell, 2017).

Jane Burbank and Frederick Cooper, *Empires in World History: Power and the Politics of Difference* (Princeton: Princeton University Press, 2010).

David S. Doddington and Enrico Dal Lago, eds., *Writing the History of Slavery* (London: Bloomsbury Academic, 2022).

David Eltis et al., *The Cambridge World History of Slavery*, 4 vols. (Cambridge: Cambridge University Press, 2011–22).

Moses I. Finley, *Ancient Slavery and Modern Ideology* (London: Chatto and Windus, 1980).

Jeff Fynn-Paul and Damian A. Pargas, eds., *Slaving Zones, Cultural Identities, Ideologies, Institutions in the Evolution of Global Slavery* (Leiden: Brill, 2018).

Paulin Ismard and Benedetta R. C. Vidal, eds., *Les Mondes de L'Esclavage: Une Historie Comparée* (Paris: Seul, 2021).

Noel Lemski and Catherine M. Cameron, eds., *What Is a Slave Society? The Practice of Slavery in Global Perspective* (Cambridge: Cambridge University Press, 2018).

Joseph C. Miller, *The Problem of Slavery as History: A Global Approach* (New Haven: Yale University Press, 2013).

Damian Pargas and Juliane Schiel, *The Palgrave Handbook of Global Slavery through History* (Basingstoke: Palgrave Macmillan, 2023).

Orlando Patterson, *Slavery and Social Death: A Comparative Study* (Cambridge, MA: Harvard University Press, 1982).

Sophie White and Trevor Burnard, eds., *Hearing Slaves' Voices: African and Indian Slave Testimony in British and French America, 1700–1848* (London: Routledge, 2020).

Michael Zeuske, *Handbuch Geschichte der Sklaverei: Eine Globalgeshichte von den Anfongen bis zur Gegenwart*, 2nd ed. (Berlin: De Gruyter, 2019).

Cambridge Elements ☰

Historical Theory and Practice

Daniel Woolf
Queen's University, Ontario

Daniel Woolf is Professor of History at Queen's University, where he served for ten years as Principal and Vice-Chancellor, and has held academic appointments at a number of Canadian universities. He is the author or editor of several books and articles on the history of historical thought and writing, and on early modern British intellectual history, including most recently *A Concise History of History* (CUP 2019). He is a Fellow of the Royal Historical Society, the Royal Society of Canada, and the Society of Antiquaries of London. He is married with 3 adult children.

About the Series
Cambridge Elements in Historical Theory and Practice is a series intended for a wide range of students, scholars, and others whose interests involve engagement with the past. Topics include the theoretical, ethical, and philosophical issues involved in doing history, the interconnections between history and other disciplines and questions of method, and the application of historical knowledge to contemporary global and social issues such as climate change, reconciliation and justice, heritage, and identity politics.

Cambridge Elements ⁼

Historical Theory and Practice

Elements in the Series

A full series listing is available at: www.cambridge.org/EHTP.

Printed in the United States
by Baker & Taylor Publisher Services